A MANUAL OF SELF-HELP *and* SELF-EMPOWERMENT *for the* 21ST CENTURY.

From the Esoteric Perspective.

JOSEPH M.MCKEANEY

BALBOA.
PRESS

A DIVISION OF HAY HOUSE

Balboa Press books may be ordered through booksellers or by contacting:

Balboa Press
A Division of Hay House
1663 Liberty Drive
Bloomington, IN 47403
www.balboapress.com
1 (877) 407-4847

Because of the dynamic nature of the Internet, any web addresses or links contained in this book may have changed since publication and may no longer be valid. The views expressed in this work are solely those of the author and do not necessarily reflect the views of the publisher, and the publisher hereby disclaims any responsibility for them.

The author of this book does not dispense medical advice or prescribe the use of any technique as a form of treatment for physical, emotional, or medical problems without the advice of a physician, either directly or indirectly. The intent of the author is only to offer information of a general nature to help you in your quest for emotional and spiritual well-being. In the event you use any of the information in this book for yourself, which is your constitutional right, the author and the publisher assume no responsibility for your actions.

Any people depicted in stock imagery provided by Thinkstock are models, and such images are being used for illustrative purposes only.
Certain stock imagery © Thinkstock.

Print information available on the last page.

ISBN: 978-1-5043-8835-1 (sc)
ISBN: 978-1-5043-8836-8 (e)

Balboa Press rev. date: 10/31/2017

THE ANCIENT SCIENCE OF ALCHEMY
IN CRYPTIC FORM:

'Thou shalt separate the Earth from the fire, the subtle from the subtle from the gross, gently and with great industry. It rises from the Earth to the heaven, and again it descends from heaven to Earth, and it receives the power of things above and of below. By this means shalt thou obtain the glory of the whole world, and all darkness shall depart from thee!'

-Hermes Trismegristus. (1)

The original spiritual science upon the Earth was called Alchemy, but not the misguided alchemy of the metal-workers during the middle-ages: it was the original science of energies for the transformation of man. Many references to it are hidden in various locations throughout the Earth ... including the hieroglyphs of ancient Egypt and the Vatican archives.

LAKOTA INDIAN PRAYER

"Teach me how to trust my heart, my mind, my intuition; my inner-knowing, the senses of my body, the blessings of my spirit.

Teach me to trust these things so that I may enter my sacred space and love beyond my fear, and thus walk in balance with the passing of each glorious Sun."

-Internet Quote

Self-Empowerment

Contents

Introduction

This module has been designed to provide an approach to self-empowerment for the individual. This self-empowerment module has been built around the esoteric perspective; self-knowledge and inner-work will lead to more and more inner-power. Inner-power emanates from the core of our being, and not from personality.

> *'Much inner-work creates a sweet Essence.' Sarmoung Sufi Saying.*

Inner-power means, ones inner qualities and working in co-operation with others, not in competition with others. It also means self-knowledge, deep understanding and sensitivity. Without self-knowledge and working on our Being, this inner-power is not possible.

External-power means essentially 'power over': others, situations, our environment etc. It does not require that we go within; explore our inner-world. External power often involves exploitation, creating fear, using others against their will. External power can be ruthless and without any semblance of conscience.

> *'Dominating power seeks out the weaknesses of others and trades upon it; inner power looks for other people's strengths and relies on them.'*
>
> *Scilla Elworthy. ... Power & Sex.*

We will focus for the most part on the subject of inner-power; the path to self-empowerment is really that of inner-power. Refusing to exploit and harm others, avoiding profiting through some one else's abject loss. The development of wisdom, conscience and sensitivity to others and to other creatures on Earth.

> *'The masculine principle began to prevail – logical thinking, scientific enquiry, rationality and 'realism' became stronger and stronger, especially in the West.*
>
> *'Over the past few centuries we have gone too far this way – too far into increasing disrespect for and destruction of the natural world, aided and hastened by technological discoveries and an impoverishment of spiritual life. People may in many ways now be more conscious and more aware, but at the same time they are cut off from the natural and the spiritual world. Our minds are alive, but our bodies and spirits are starved and dying. We may be clever, but we are out of balance.'*
>
> Scilla Elworthy. … Power & Sex.

It is significant to understand that inner-power does not preclude external power; save that, an individual with true inner-power will never manifest external power in the ways mentioned above. Only balanced and just external power can be manifested by a person with authentic inner-power.

In this module, we will look at self-knowledge, self-exploration and real inner change, from a backdrop of how our outer personalities have become infected by a highly mechanical and profit-driven society. We will study methods of self-empowerment, through principles and techniques developed over millennia and handed down to us through a chain-of-transmission, from esoteric schools and authentic teachers.

This is a journey of self-discovery, one which will require that we look to the hidden powers of our inner-being (Essence), and work with Sincerity, Humility, Courage & Tenacity. We must work on our inner potentials!

Our task is essentially to learn more about ourselves, our weaknesses and our strengths, without shrinking from them. Then we must endeavour to increase our strengths and abilities through self-knowledge, whilst always decreasing our dark side or weaknesses.

> 'Man's obligation is to co-operate with the laws which operate the universe. Because man has a unique place, the obligation goes with that.

> 'The awareness of your place is not a gift of Nature. You must find it by conscious effort, not by hope. Man has a potentiality he knows nothing about. This forms the science of ancient times. We have lost all idea of these potentialities.'

> **G.I. Gurdjieff.** *(2)*

Advice From The Writer

We are not accustomed to think of life in terms of self-empowerment; coming into our power and living an authentic life - we are more geared towards materialistic accomplishments and pursuits!

However, to understand life and the meaning of our existence, we have to use something other than intellectual capacity and ordinary societal standards - we must use our natural inborn cognitive ability. It must be said here, not everyone possess this today, since it is, for the most part, submerged in our sub-consciousness. The number of people with a heightened ability in this sphere are very few indeed, and we do not meet such people every day.

Intellectual capacity refers to scholastic pursuits, academia, mechanistic contemporary science, learning by rote, contemporary 'education' etc.

Cognitive ability on the other hand, is connected with profound perception, penetrating vision of the human condition and potentialities, awareness of higher knowledge and cosmic dimensions other than the mundane.

To see the human condition clearly and without the all-pervasive 'societal-fog' that seems to be ever present in today's societies, one must have a higher than average cognitive level. We can develop a higher cognitive level through the study of esoteric materials. That is, high level esoteric literature such as that which G.I Gurdjieff and P.D. Ouspensky gave us in the last century … a treasure-trove of powerful and authentic wisdom, from a bygone Age.

This type of literature provides us with a profound insight into the human condition - beyond academia, science, sociology and history. It also illuminates a Path, which is today elusive and invisible to the average person in the street; a portal to a new world of concepts, ideas, principles and practical knowledge!

This wisdom comes to us from ancient times, from a period on Earth when authentic knowledge and wisdom flourished. Since then, we have gone from wisdom to 'knowledge', and now to information - and this information is of a very partial nature. So partial, in fact, that we see the emergence of a new type of human being; people who, in real terms, know nothing. To top it all – this phenomenon is not an accident … there are more forces at work than we suspect.

What young people acquire in schools and colleges is not knowledge, it is merely a shadowy type of learning, learning with a small "l". Modern people are now so dull, they do not comprehend what this type of banal learning does to young people, and all of the subsequent consequences for the future. Thus, the cycle of crass ineptitude continues unabated.

We have become a civilization of 'compliant clones', without integrity, authenticity or a definitive purpose in life. Most people today 'blow with the prevailing wind', without principles, insight, foresight or a code of ethics. Those things which should be taught at school and by parents or guardians; are by in large missing from our contemporary cultures.

"Man is 99% social animal, only 1% himself." -G.I. Gurdjieff.

What's more, its mere child's play to demonstrate this - it is certainly not 'rocket science'. It is with this backdrop that we find ourselves, and it is within this context that we must work against the mechanical current in life - to empower ourselves. We cannot empower ourselves via antiquated and outmoded 'educational' modalities. Yes, we may obtain, wealth, status, power, money, and position in society, but this is not self-empowerment in a true and authentic sense. What is inside, remains immature, ignorant, spoilt and conceited. Without a specific line of work on ourselves, we will sadly hover between ignorance and an over inflated vision of ourselves.

This all important line of work is now completely missing from our schools and colleges – it no longer exists in our contemporary cultures.

All of the above **has become invisible** to contemporary people; we can no longer perceive, as strange, what has become the norm for us, in our daily lives. We believe ourselves to possess qualities, abilities and a host of perceptions – we simply do not possess. The **race consciousness** is a vast homogenous-pit, from which few escape. It devours everyone and everything in its path, creating lifeless automatons, and vast numbers of people who never learn to think for themselves – all created and marshalled via a 'top-down' and highly contrived 'education' system, in sterile environments called classrooms or lecture-halls. Unfortunately, this is no exaggeration – having studied this paradigm closely for thirty years now, it is obvious to me that we live in a system designed to direct people's minds in a very specific direction and away from any form of Truth or higher-reality. To the modern mind-set this seems absurd, but it is a paradox; modern peoples are thoroughly brainwashed and can no longer perceive that which they are 'thoroughly soaked in' – ignorance dressed-up as knowledge.

Just as the goldfish that swims around in a glass-bowl, has no knowledge of the ocean, and has no idea that its whole existence is spent in a totally artificial environment; similarly, we who live in artificial and contrived social structures, have no inkling that our lives have become so boring, so limited and so unnatural, that it is a miracle that we continue as we do, and not rebel. We live under the illusion of freedom but possess no real freedom whatsoever.

> 'Our culture has bred consumers and addicts. We eat too much, buy too much, and want too much. We set ourselves on the fruitless mission of filling the gaping hole within us, with material things. Blindly, we consume more and more, believing we are hungry for more food, status or money, yet really we are hungry for connection.'

> -Vironika Tugaleva. Internet.

The reason for this, is because our brainwashing is so complete and hermetically sealed; we do not question those elements in life which are so important to our advancement as intelligent beings, but merely acquiesce in the notion that we must focus on material possessions, power, comfort, convenience and pleasure. Anything outside of these basics, we ignore as unnecessary, excessive or unobtainable. We lack the requisite intelligence to see what we are losing! **This realization is unavoidable, once we**

investigate what is happening in our culture today – up close and with ruthless honesty: upon obtaining a higher cognitive level in ourselves!

In some respects, this makes self-empowerment more difficult - we must work to change our artificial disposition; our immersion in the race-consciousness. Only by working to destroy linear and stereotypical thinking, and to remove societal conditioning in ourselves, can we hope to break free from a conformist and restrictive paradigm we call society.

We are willing slaves, mainly because we know no other way - our experience and knowledge are both very limited, although we constantly live under the illusion of 'being in the know' and possessing 'gold-standard' educational instruction. We are crammed full of vacuous educational clap-trap, with little or no emotional development to our nature. This is a disaster for modern peoples because it limits the full and proper development of a human being – we have become a race of superficial people, with only an absurd and banal training behind us in our school years, and no inkling of how to bring up our own children to exhibit qualities of compassion, sensitivity, vision, love, understanding, supportiveness of others, joy, creativity and positive communication. **We know what is necessary but have no idea how to obtain for our children, that which we truly wish for them.**

Schools and colleges now destroy most of these abilities and qualities in young people; they are a collective of lost people, turning to drugs and other such pharmaceutical substances to get through the gauntlet of college or University! What we are witnessing before our very eyes, is a complete travesty – a 'six- hundred-pound-gorilla in our living room' that everyone ignores. It is, of course, ignored because of **fear**, people are afraid to be out of step with the System. The two great controlling factors at work constantly in our culture – fear and brainwashing – we are surrounded by these toxic factors, invisible to the majority of onlookers!

It all comes back to **the structure** and **ethos** of our culture - so long as we have a primitive modus operandi of greed, banal competition, damaging medicines produced by the big pharmaceutical companies, teachers and mentors who themselves have no inner-qualities – that can be transmitted to students, government realpolitik, fear and naked aggression between nations and indeed, between communities within nation States, we are not going anywhere.

We are naïve when it comes to pharmaceutical medicines and vaccines, our programming on these is almost complete – we are not conscious of how dangerous many of these really are:

"The medical authorities keep lying. Vaccination has been a disaster on the immune system. It causes lots of illness. We are actually changing our gentic code through vaccination. Vaccination is the biggest crime against humanity."

-Doctor G.Lanctot. M.D. Canada.

We are like little children, accepting all and everything the medical profession propose or give out – this is a highly dangerous situation. However, more and more people are beginning to wake up to the corrupt practices in medicine around the world – controlled by a half-a-dozen mega-corporations.

"As a retired physician, I can honestly say that unless you are in a serious accident, you best chance of living to a ripe old age is to avoid doctors and hospitals and learn nutrition, herbal medicine and other forms of natural medicine; unless you are fortunate enough to have a naturopathic physician available. Almost all drugs are toxic and are designed to treat symptoms and not the cause anymore."

-Doctor Allan Greenberg M.D. fb / SacredEarth 1.

In this manual, I hope to explore the numerous dynamics involved with self-empowerment within modern societies; especially so, from the esoteric perspective.

I think it is safe to say that most people do not fully understand this concept of self-empowerment. Although people will affirm their comprehension, quite often, it is really very vague, and has no bearing on authentic self-empowerment. The vast majority of people are so pre-occupied with earning money; careers, business, parenting, 'eduaction' etc. that they fail to be concerned with their own development and empowerment. This attitude is, of course, myopic in the extreme.

We cannot be complete as human beings, if we merely work, spend, pro-create and die. This is not what human life was intended to be. It is a degradation of our humanity to merely remain a 'small cog' in a very large and meaningless mechanism - known as society.

Empowerment is simply a natural progression: it is a natural movement towards authenticity, awareness, sensitivity, and inner-power. This phase in life in necessary, if we are to develop naturally and holistically as human beings. **The structure and ethos of modern cultures now serves to restrict and retard authentic forms of self-cultivation and self-empowerment. This is a major blind-spot in contemporary sociology and psychology.**

It is not a luxury or a prestige, it is more an organic outgrowth - a phase in human life, which is found in an embryonic state in practically each and every person. The exceptions being those people who have various types of personality-disorders, which have increased in the population over the past twenty-five years, or so.

Personality disorders block the development of self-empowerment; since the psyche has become abnormal and imbalanced to the degree, whereby a natural progression in the inner unfoldment becomes impossibe. A good example of this is the narcissist.

THE NARCISSIST

The narcissist wishes to control, to acquire power over others by whatever means are at hand. To this end, they will focus on the small weaknesses of others, seeking out their 'Achilles heel', so this can be used to undermine their target or targets. Egoism is the key element at play here, and this egoism is the chief protagonist in the creation of chaos in our society.

A balanced and natural person will focus on the good qualities and abilities of another - relating to others in a very positive way, without malice, hubris or egoism. <u>Seeking out the weakness of another in order to exploit it, is ignorance on a new level and can never have a positive result for either party</u>.

Unfortunately, not so with the narcissist, they are happiest when intrigue, deception and gossip are afoot. They like to engage in sabotage, blocking- manoeuvres, character-assassination, and other malicious social patterns.

Many people we may simply see as individuals with odd behaviour may actually be narcissists - they tend to cloak their bad behaviour until something triggers tantrums, sabotage, blocking patterns or opposition.

The chief facet of a narcissist, is that of their propensity to use others. They wish to gain, if necessary, through the loss of others. They tend to be attracted to certain jobs or career paths, where they can exercise control over others. This, then, provides an open doorway to exploit and sometimes humiliate people - they consider lesser mortals.

These types, see self-empowerment as acquisition and material in nature. They are not interested in the development of new qualities, abilities and integrity in themselves. They view this as a non-starter and a waste of time. Integrity is not high on their list of aims.

THE STEPS NECESSARY TO START THE PROCESS OF SELF-EMPOWERMENT

* **Stepping outside the herd mentality. Becoming aware of our own conditioning within society.**
* **Awareness that the trite conformity of society is disempowering.**
* **However, non-conformity is not enough – something else is needed!**
* **Becoming aware of *psychohomeostasis* or cognitive dissonance.**
* **[That which we are afraid to investigate becomes our limitation]**
* **Understanding that intellectual capacity does not equal cognitive ability …. one may have a high intellectual capacity, yet still have a low cognitive ability.**
* **The understanding that one must become rounded in one's inner inner-development, and that all things truly valuable come only with effort.**
* **Becoming aware that nobody is interested in your inner-development: except you.**
* **Understanding the dynamics of society, and how people are subtly brainwashed by societal forces, and why there is**

essentially no actual individuation or separate, objective intelligence, existing within our society. Rather, people merely reflect the consensus-reality or race-consciousness by mimicking others!

* Going beyond the highly restrictive and limited race consciousness is essential to self-empowerment and authenticity.
* Using esoteric wisdom and the highly valuable principles and ideas found therein, can facilitate a new path to profound understanding, and techniques for self-empowerment, unavailable elsewhere.
* Becoming aware that self-motivation is key to all empowerment and developing the ability to self-motivate.

WHAT SELF-EMPOWERMENT IS NOT:

* Riches.
* Prestige.
* Fame.
* Position.
* Style.
* Social Abilities and Skills.
* Authority Figures.
* Being a Brilliant Orator.
* Business Acumen.
* Artistic Ability.
* Musical Ability.
* Physical Attributes.
* Sexual Prowess.
* A Brilliant Sense of Humour.
* Career Success.
* Well Travelled.
* A Strong Personality.
* Wealth.
* Influence.
* Power.

The societal view of power is, of course, that of external-power or 'power-over' ... the more power we have over others, the less work we have to do ourselves; so there is the illusion of power. But this is not authentic power, it is merely 'the shadow of real power'. Real power comes from within. It is not an external phenomenon as we generally understand it. However, if a person has inner-power, it is reflected in a positive fashion all around such an individual. There, one will find great positivity, flexibility, wisdom and a sharp intelligence. Violence and cohersion will be absent from such an equation - instead, one will witness co-operation, unity of purpose, support, felicity and a lack of greed.

All real power is based on such principles ... love, wisdom, positive creativity, insight, sensitivity, awareness and integrity. However, many are the number of people who believe greed, anger and violence are the keys to a successful life!

WHAT SELF-EMPOWERMENT IS:

* Astuteness.
* A Sense of Purpose.
* A Positive Attitude to Life and to Others.
* Positive Communication at all Times.
* Integrity.
* Wisdom.
* Respect for Others.
* Awareness.
* Self-Motivation.
* Tact.
* A Sense of Humour Geared towards Alleviating Suffering of Others.
* Compassion.
* Flexibility.
* A Hard-Working Attitude.
* True Intelligence as Opposed to Intellectual Capacity and Academia.
* Resourcefulness.
* Positive Determination.

* **A High Cognitive Ability.**
* **A True Sense of Humility.**
* **A Sense of Inclusiveness.**
* **Bravery.**
* **Authentic Confidence - Not Bravado.**
* **Natural Self-Esteem.**
* **The Ability to see 'the Big Picture' and beyond mere externals.**

"It is the Flowering of Love,
That ends the Spell of Reason.
And we Begin to Observe Reality,
Beyond the Outer Forms."
- Rumi.

Disempowered People

We live in an Age of disempowered people, individuals who do not think for themselves, who think the State will look after their needs, who essentially feel that they have no adjustment to make in their own development.

> 'People who feel they have no need to change, let them sleep.' - Rumi.

The art of living, is truly the **art of self-empowerment**, and it is an art which must be exercised whilst empowering others. Become a beacon of light for others, illuminating their way, demonstrating tangibly, what is possible for an individual to achieve.

People view wealthy or powerful individuals in society and think this is empowerment, but it is merely external, very often no inner-change has taken place whatever. These people become 'powerful things', without genuine human qualities and without authentic human intelligence. As Gurdjieff tells us in his writings, we have become automatons – with only automatic-reason, a mind-set focused on the pleasure principle, pseudo-science, self-gratification and egoism. Humility and honour has become scarce in our modern day cultures – we no longer value integrity, wisdom, insight and vision.

> 'If you still believe what you've been taught to believe is true without researching, then it's proof that your brainwashing was successful.'
>
> -Internet quote

When No Inner-Change is Present

When no inner-change has been effected in a person, what does it really mean? What is the real difference in a person with authentic inner growth, and a person without any such development?

Let us take the individual with no inner-development whatever, but lives in alignment with that which surrounds him or her - completely. Such a person will manifest the race-consciousness in almost all situations and in how they relate to others. They will carry all the usual prejudices, mental and emotional habits, forms of thinking and constant comparison, hubris, conceit, egoism and feelings of superiority or perhaps inferiority to others in their environment. **Egoism replaces compassion, sensitivity and insight.**

They will spend time in gossip, worrying about world affairs, politics, their neighbour's disputes and all the minutiae in life which drain time and their attention. They will thrive on television and spurious internet psychobabble, conspiracy theories which have zero foundation - unable to spot the real gems present in such accounts, for they have no powers of discrimination.. **!**

On the other hand, the individual with real inner-power or genuine empowerment, will shine qualities of individuality, non-compliance with restrictive conservative cultures, the ability to 'think outside the box', non-alignment with politics or pseudo-cultural activities. They will manifest personal qualities of resilience, courage, awareness, sensitivity, tact, genuine compassion for others, and an intelligence outside of the herd-mentality.

And here is the conundrum for today's spiritually developed and super-aware people - one cannot be such, and comply with social norms and trite conventions ... in other words, if we are totally aware spiritually, it also means we are totally aware of what is happening all around us in society; if we are thus aware of all the fake and sometimes dangerous modalities in society, in a profound way, we are then abdicating our integrity and duty to ourselves if we take part in them mechanically - as if we are blind.

However, such is the pressure of societal forces in today's world, that many aware people put their collective heads in the sand - Ostrich style. Fear, and the desire to remain within a comfort-zone and to conform, often carries the day - a very large proportion of 'aware people' fall into this category.

Those people who are perhaps in the top ten percent of super-aware people, are not concerned with a comfort-zone, nor are they worried about the opinions of others; including friends and family members. To these people, integrity of thought and action is paramount, and they strive for parity between their principles, motivations and how they act. They will not be deterred by the prevailing paradigm of the day, by societal mores or defunct ideas. **They are a different calibre of person** ... unconcerned by the many obstacles thrown up by lesser minds, unperturbed by the sabotage of individuals jealous of their profound dignity and purpose. These people are not to be trifled-with.

> *"Maturity is learning to walk away from people and situations that threaten your peace of mind, self-respect, values, morals and self-worth."*

> - Working Women ... Internet Quote.

Destiny

Our true destiny as human beings, is that of self-empowerment via wisdom and perseverance. Nothing is achieved without work - we can easily deceive ourselves, but at the end of the day, nothing worthwhile acquiring or achieving for oneself and others, comes to us gratis.

What we achieve through the herd-mentality is not empowerment - it is merely a form of slavery and abject disempowerment. This is for many 'a hard pill to swallow', but nonetheless it is the truth of the matter. We see today, that people generally do not want Truth, but seek comfort & convenience, etc.

Because people hide from Truth in today's world, nothing resembling Truth is ever taken on board - people live in a small 'bubble' of their own narrow self-interest.

Added to this, we have the phenomenon of *minimal-retention*. I discovered this particular phenomenon while teaching European students esoteric ideas and esoteric principles in London ... these students were from a wide ranging background and from various European countries. They found it difficult to retain these arcane ideas, and had to revise regularly the materials we covered together. Later I discovered, this phenomenon is directly connected to the development of neural pathways in the brain. When a person is immersed in the mundane activities of everyday life - certain definitive neural pathways are developed in the brain of such a person. On the other hand, when one studies esoteric materials with intention and with great purpose, different neural pathways are developed in one's brain. These new neural pathways unfortunately tend to recede, when we go back into the mechanical hum-drum of ordinary life; we tend to slowly lose what we have gained or what we have understood. So, it is necessary to reinforce our esoteric study habits with regular immersion in this incredible subject.

Not only this, but we must put into practice everything we have learned and all we have come to understand - this is a must if we are to hold onto what we have discovered. The blessings are many and great, for those who are determined, motivated and persevere. **In ancient times, it was deemed a duty for the individual to study and understand Cosmic Truth**, today we are in a state of amnesia, our focus is so convoluted and naïve, that, without proper training, we are a lost and confused. The nature of Cosmic Truth eludes us, and we go on suffering as before – not having developed any understanding of life.

Only through putting into practice what we have learned, can we hone our intelligence and skills in life. Only by this means, can we develop new and positive qualities in ourselves and rid ourselves of faults, negative attitudes and negative behaviour. Our fate in many ways lies in our own hands - we can be master of our own destiny, but only if we are humble and sincere enough to value what esoteric wisdom is?

Sufi Saying

It is not what one knows but what we truly understand,
It is not what we can remember,
But what we can make use of in everyday life!

Today, the vast majority of people value material things, kudos, power, prestige, wealth etc. but **do not value authentic knowledge and wisdom. They will make any sacrifice or payment you care to mention for material things or power, but for wisdom they do not wish to work or pay for!** This is because people are asleep when it comes to knowledge, and mistake the pale and jaded information and academia they are given at school for knowledge. Schools and colleges are teaching outdated and anachronistic materials to a compliant and simple-minded audience of students. Students who do not know **how to think for themselves** but are eager to obtain the requisite 'passports' to access a jobs market predicated on these certificates or degrees. Thus, the carnival of ineptitude and stupidity continues as if it were 'knowledge of a different order', we are continuously duped by a system that has been honed and perfected over hundreds of years – compliance and acceptance over hundreds of years is a very powerful means of controlling the masses.

Learning by rote, vast amounts of dead and infantile materials is not learning. Yet, contemporary people will 'defend to the death' such modern institutes as schools, colleges, Universities, pharmaceutical medicines, psychiatry, vaccinations, etc. Sadly, the vast majority of people have no idea how they are continually lied to – once trust is gained from the collective, it is very easy to slip lies and counterfeit ideas under their radar!

"One half of the world does not know how the other half lies!"
G.I. Gurdjieff.

Nowadays, people behave more like sheep, than like free-thinking human beings; who possess insight, vision and the ability to perceive and sense reality.

> *"Man's possibilities are very great. You cannot conceive of a shadow of what man is capable of attaining. But nothing can be attained in sleep. In the consciousness of a sleeping man, his illusions, his 'dreams' are mixed with his reality. He lives in a subjective world and can never escape from it. This is the reason he can never make use of all the powers he possesses and why he lives in only a small part of himself."*

> G.I. Gurdjieff.

Different Levels Of Empowerment

There is no single level of empowerment in this world; it is a multi-level paradigm. It goes beyond our very limited level of conception - there are higher levels of self-empowerment which provide a platform to take us into dimensions of higher consciousness and higher Being, as the ancients of our world clearly understood. This is not comprehended by modern man.

However, the first stages of this vast and exciting process, involves a new-found confidence, expanded self-esteem, a heightened-vision, a strong impulse to help others, compassion in one's actions, a positive attitude to life, love and the acquiring of new abilities and skills; on the physical, emotional, psychological and spiritual levels.

The foundations of which, must be built before this structure of empowerment manifests in full. It is a long process, predicated upon intelligence and vision.

> *"One of the marvels of the world, is the sight of a soul sitting in prison with the key in its hand."*

> - Rumi.

The Secret To Self-Empowerment

The great secret to this, is that, the 'blueprint' for all inner-unfoldment already exists within each of us. In other words, the potential exists for this development in the majority people, it is just necessary to bring it out.

The key to this is, of course, motivation; having the necessary motivation, which essentially must be self-motivation, without which we cannot progress.

Motivation comes from a clear understanding of what is possible, and also the efforts necessary to manifest these possibilities: hard-work and intelligence are necessary; then great things are possible.

> *"If a man becomes too polished by modern education, it becomes impossible for him to approach Truth or esoteric teachings."*

> G.I. Gurdjieff.

The Empowered Human

Here, I will outline the basic level of empowerment for men and women. It is always connected to elevated human intelligence, which is not as many believe, an increased intellectual or academic capacity - rather it is an expanded cognitive ability or **true intelligence** in human beings.

An empowered person will always come from integrity, compassion and from truth. They very often have left the race-consciousness behind - resting in awareness, sensitivity, courage, tenacity and deep understanding. This ethos is often found to be tempered by an ancient wisdom from a bygone time.

This type of intelligence is far superior to intellectual capacity, and cannot be acquired within our current pseudo-educational systems! However, because of the brainwashing which has occurred on a vast scale, the adherence to modern modes of learning and life-patterns predicated upon materialism and wealth; we no longer value the spiritual path – personal qualities and arcane wisdom!

> *"Modern education is a form of imposed ignorance." - Noam Chomsky.*

The difference Between Intellectual Capacity and Cognitive Ability

This item is of vast importance and has incredible implications with regards self-empowerment and one's inner-development.

> *"Your time is limited, so don't waste it on living someone else's life. Don't be trapped by dogma – which is living with the results of other people's thinking. Don't let the noise of other's*

opinions drown out your inner voice. And most important, have the courage to follow your heart and intuition."

-Steve Jobs. [Stanford Address]

Intellectual capacity is what society subsists on, it is the aim and modus operandi of all modern mechanistic 'education'. It is considered to be the ultimate path for contemporary peoples; we can see this in the universities and colleges, with doctors and psychiatrists etc. etc. The arrogance, the conceit, and people who very often consider themselves 'untouchable' and outside the remit of all 'other mortals' ... A class set apart, you will understand what I mean, if you are a 'hands on' and a real person, a person who questions on a deep structured level, that which is all around us - otherwise not!

Bahaudin Naqshband

'The people called scholars are appalled at two things; first they do not like the methods which we use to reach the ears of people, because they think that what has to be communicated must be done either by intimidation or by complicated terminology. They are appalled by another thing: that we are said to be hostile to scholars.

But the reality is very different. The people who are called scholars are substitutes for scholars. There are few real scholars, and a superabundance of these other people.

As a result, they have acquired the generic name of scholars. In countries where there are no horses, donkeys are called horses.'

Wisdom of the East – Idries Shah.

This, attitude displayed by numerous so called professionals today, is merely illusion on a vast scale, ignorance and hubris dressed up in self-importance. In reality, it is comical ... seeing these types so full to the brim of self-importance and self-conceit. The truth is, they know very little, and possess little or no development of their own Being, and are not embarrassed by same!

What is not understood by contemporary people, is that intellectual capacity does not equate to real intelligence ... to cognitive ability. Real intelligence is something other than intellect and academia. However, such is the all- pervasive conditioning and programming in contemporary societies – people cannot grasp this even if has been explained to them in some detail.

Intellectual capacity is concerned with scholastic-pursuits, academia, abstract study such as mathematics, learning by rote, memorizing 'facts', history, profane science, contemporary schools where basically one is taught information and very little real knowledge or wisdom.

Young people leave these institutions often damaged and without any authentic emotional development or maturity. They have very often low confidence and self-esteem and poor communication skills. Neither does modern education engender motivation in our young people, other than the tardy motivation to acquire material wealth and material things. We rarely see the conveying of real integrity, excellence in behaviour, respect for others, clarity of thought and action. We continuously see our young lost and frightened when they finish school .... with one-third of young people in the U.S are addicted to drugs; pharmaceutical drugs - prescribed at their schools.

> *"But from the very beginning we start corrupting every child with the poison of competitiveness. By the time he comes out of university he will be completely poisoned. We have hypnotized him with the idea that he has to fight with others, that life is the survival of the fittest."*

> *"A real education will not teach you to compete; it will teach you to cooperate. It will not teach you to fight and come first. It will teach you to be creative, to be loving, to be blissful, without comparing yourself to others. It will not teach you that you can be happy only when you are first – that is sheer nonsense. You can't be happy just by being first; and in trying*

to be first you go through such misery that by the time you become the first you are habituated to misery."

JOY – The Happiness that Comes from Within: Osho.

We also witness the dumbing down of education in the U.S. - which began around a hundred years ago. Plutocrats and those in power decided to render education in the U.S. basically null and void, by purposely removing key issues, knowledge and instruction to students. Curiously, most youth today have not even noticed this phenomenon – they remain completely ignorant of it!

It should be noted here for the sake of completeness, that the U.S. is not the only country where this has taken place, most other countries have followed suit. It is now endemic or what one might call the norm.

When certain key facets of information and knowledge are removed from the populace, it lends itself to lowering the collective cognitive ability of the masses. Intellectual capacity increases, but authentic cognitive ability or **real intelligence** is forfeited.

This phenomenon is not by any means an accident, as the naive always think ... it is clearly by design. The powers that be do not wish to have a population of super-intelligent people, this would not fit with their plans and certainly, they would not be able to execute many of their civic policies and hyper-taxation agendas if it were so.

> *"You are in the process of being indoctrinated. We have not evolved a system of education, that is not a system of indoctrination. What you are being taught here is an amalgam of current prejudice and the choices of this particular culture. The slightest look at history will show how impermanent these must be."*

> - Doris Lessing: 2007 Nobel Prize Winner for Literature.

And, strangely enough, it is mere child's play to demonstrate that this took place around a century ago. We find the industrialists and the societal elite, who at that time controlled vast numbers of people through having

13

them as their workforce in factories etc. did not hide their intentions and modus operandi in this respect. They spoke of controlling the education system to their own liking and to their own ends openly and with great alacrity.

> *"In our dreams, people yield themselves with perfect docility to our molding hands."* [Schooling the World by Carol Black]

> John D. Rockerfeller. General Education Board 1906.
> U.S.A.

With a little research we can discover the 'fingerprints' of the powers that be all over our current education system ... it is not at all what it should be! **Our modern education teaches young people what to think and not how to think.**

> *'A general State education is a mere contrivance for moulding people to be exactly like one another: and as the mould in which it is casts them is that which pleases the predominant power in the government ... it establishes a despotism over the mind, leading by a natural tendency to one over the body.'*

> John Stuart Mill. 'On Liberty. [Schooling the World Video-Documentary]

> - By Carol Black.

On the other hand, cognitive ability is connected with seeing the big-picture, perceiving profound Cosmic Truth, awareness which reflects deeply on oneself and one's position in the cosmos. Cognitive ability, when enhanced in us, brings clarity, deeper perception, sensitivity, precision of thought, lucidity, creativity and a new awareness of potentialities for oneself and others.

Cognitive awareness can contribute to the development of integrity and other human qualities in the individual .... intellectual capacity and academia do not!

"Our schools are, in a sense, factories, in which the raw materials – children – are being shaped and fashioned into products.

The specifications for manufacturing come from the demands of 20th century civilization, and it is the business of the school to build pupils according to the specifications laid down,"

Ellwood P. Cubberly. Dean of Stanford University. School of Education. 1898.

[Schooling the World - by Carol Black]

Cognitive Awareness Continued

This is a much bigger subject than one might at first imagine; much can be gleaned from being able to differentiate between these two aspects in man's cognitive instrument.

Contemporary society considers intellectual capacity to be the pinnacle of modern man's achievement and advancement. However, this is a crass presumption on our part. In reality, it is merely the first level, in a very large 'pyramid' of cognitive levels and potentialities. This has been known, for example, by the Sufis for thousands of years ... bearing in mind that Sufism, by the real meaning of that word [those who are on the Path] have existed long before the advent of the Islamic religion, and of the Islamic prophet.

Greater and Lesser Sufism

To clarify the above, there are two distinct types of Sufis to be found in the world. The first called the lesser Sufis, teach that one must access Truth and Wisdom via religion, and in this case usually the Islamic religion. The second type of Sufism is that of the Greater Sufis – they stress that one does not need the medium of any religion to approach the true Path of Wisdom!

In the West, we normally encounter the religious Sufis, and as a result often presume that it is an off-shoot of Islam, or that it has no appeal to our knowledge oriented mind-set. For many people, what we are actually looking for is the Greater Sufism!

We are unaware as contemporary people, just how far we can develop our cognitive level. We are thoroughly conditioned to see intellectual capacity as everything, and nothing worthwhile existing beyond this!

An increased and enhanced cognitive ability, is merely the first level of a vast 'stairway of possibilities'; levels of intelligence and consciousness we find mentioned in the ground-breaking works of 'In Search of the Miraculous' by P.D. Ouspensky and, 'All and everything' by George Ivanovitch Gurdjieff.

Modern man is unaware that collectively, our cognitive level has diminished over vast spans of time. We have become addicted to the concepts of the intellect and that of academia: like 'kids in a toy-shop' ... not aware that more sophisticated and amazing instruments and machines exist in the world.

The key to life is in reality, our cognitive level, which means, the higher it has developed in us, the more integrated our psyche, or one could say more accurately - our centres [chakras]. With a heightened cognitive ability, we begin to see beyond the normal stereotyped vision of things - we begin to see how war and violence are useless and evil, we begin to understand the importance of knowledge of a different order; of wisdom which was once possessed by the ancient civilizations of our world.

The Core Paradox for the Contemporary Mind-Set

Upon close scrutiny of core esoteric ideas, we encounter a paradox which presents itself to modern man, and that is:

Intellectuals are the Enemy of True Knowledge and Authentic Wisdom:

We, as contemporary people, are unaware of Knowledge existing on different levels and possessing different qualities – this lies outside the remit of our current-collective-cognitive level.

However, this is true, and modern people cannot grasp this paradigm which comes to us from esoteric wisdom – modern education being the chief culprit.

In fact, we are required to change our Being, in order to increase our cognitive level .... so that we may comprehend knowledge on higher and higher levels.

Why is this so?

Knowledge and Being:

We do not understand in contemporary times, that our knowledge depends on the level of our Being, and that there is a definitive co-relationship between these two facets of our psyche.

Should we wish to deepen and expand our knowledge, and here I am not speaking of intellectual knowledge, it is necessary simultaneously, to develop our Being. In our Western culture, we have no concept of developing our Being – it is a blind-spot in our learning and awareness. In Eastern cultures, the idiom of Being and the importance of Being-development is generally understood – not perhaps precisely, but it exists in the collective-psyche without a doubt!

A failure to expand our Being development means we stay at the level of the intellect – logic and academia. This is a core element of all authentic esoteric teaching – it is necessary to understand this before one can explore esoteric teachings for oneself.

This incursion into objective esoteric Knowledge leads to a new understanding of life, and life's possibilities. In ancient times this was represented by the Goddess Isis and elsewhere Ma'at. On temple drawings and depictions -positioned atop the head of Ma'at was the feather of Truth, and in her right hand the sacred Ankh – the Egyptian symbol of immortality for man. Both were representations of the Great Goddess – the divine feminine principle.

We begin to perceive the importance of the divine feminine principle in life, and the critical importance of women in life's equation. Our respect for women quadruples once we understand the pivotal position occupied by the feminine principle on this planet Earth. All advanced and ancient cultures of our world understood and demonstrated the importance of keeping the male and female principles in balance: both within the individual and within a culture. This crucial wisdom has been lost to us today, in contemporary times.

All spiritual work **begins** with this equal development of the masculine and feminine principles internally – this is not understood by contemporary people.

Within the average man in the street, we will find his feminine side weak and underdeveloped. This he must compensate for, if he is to become truly aware and balanced as a human being. He must cultivate in himself those precious feminine qualities, such as, sensitivity, compassion, supportiveness, kindness, simplicity of action, tact, nurturing and healing.

Within the woman, she must cultivate the strong and daring masculine traits of courage, tenacity, leadership abilities, confidence and self-esteem.

She must learn how to stand her ground and state her case without being negative, controlling or manipulative.

The development of one's own opposite pole, internally, does not create a butch woman or a soft and effeminate man – on the contrary, it cultivates a new type of human being … one that is strong, confident, balanced and humane. The resulting harmonic creates a third-force; a new intelligence is forged in the person's nature, and we see a dramatic transformation take place within that person. This is the first stage of self-empowerment for all human beings – it is one that we can accomplish for ourselves with a little instruction and a dash of encouragement.

All balance in society is derived from the recognition of the feminine and the masculine poles of life; integrating and combining these in harmony, produces a progressive and harmonic culture - devoid of struggle between the sexes, and also the absence of a lopsided cultural dynamic.

When our eyes are opened to the banal controlling influences in our current backward societies, bearing in mind that profane science and contemporary technology do not make a society - something else is needed. In reality, the collective level of Being determines the level of our societies - not the obvious march of technology, banal academia and 'creature comforts'.

We are very far from civilization, because the word civilization infers the absence of war, exploitation, greed, famine, destructive technology, bizzare and dangerous medicines, and myopic scientific methodologies. We do not have civilization, we have a system that passes for civilization … we are a lost people - immersed in self-deception and greed.

The controlling forces behind today's civilization are not coming from an evolved consciousness; they are not forces of vision, compassion, love and reciprocity. We are now on 'a runaway train' and there is no one driving - our destiny is not assured.

Our misguided feelings of security, because of belonging to a particular country or State, today, are misplaced. It is a false-security. Our civilization is of a very fragile nature because of the type and number of destructive weapons we have carelessly allowed to develop and proliferate.

Our societal lives are artificial, without substance or meaning, and without authentic direction. Our lives are based on banal repetition, and we deviate into all kinds of depravity and drug-abuse in order to alleviate the boredom and sense of emptiness. We also try to fill the void with increasingly sophisticated forms of technology and gadgets; it has become a carnival of dreams. We can never fill this void which we encounter all around us, by such means - it is an abyss of empty gestures by 'science' and by shallow governments, lacking the wisdom and understanding of how to **create and maintain harmonic and dynamic cultures.**

To do this, a different order of knowledge and wisdom is required, a modus operandi not present in today's world. We would do well to learn from those ancient cultures of our world, emulate their wisdom, their incredible dynamics, simplicity and power. We should study their healing modalities, cultural pursuits, ancient sciences, knowledge of subtle energies and stellar movements. This is without a doubt, the direction we must go in order to create a sustainable existence on planet Earth!

It is now clear from various discoveries in archaeology and anthropology around the world, that the ancient civilizations of our planet used subtle-energies and not the 'exposive-energies' we make use of today in almost all of our technology. Subtle-energies were utilized back then, because they caused zero damage to human beings and to the environment in general. Rather more intelligent than the present day modus operandi, I should think.

While hanging on to the outmoded and laughable theories of Darwinism, we fail to understand that civilizations that predated our own by thousands of years, perhaps even tens of thousands of years, knew things we do not. This is a definitive blind-spot in our modern collective consciousness; we are taken in by our own limited world view and adherence to vacuous theories, invented by dubious and eccentric characters in our own recent history. Darwin could not come to real knowledge on this subject of evolution and the nature of civilizations formerly on the Earth, simply because his Being was immature and naïve – and he had no access to esoteric knowledge! He was an individual bearing the inept stamp of his time, a time of scientific presumptions and theories, not worthy of contemporary times. Darwin is now a definitive anachronism – even though his theories are still taught across the board in many Universities and Colleges to this day! Ignorance seems to be in fashion!!

The Gradual Emergence of a New Scientific Paradigm

All discoveries in anthropology and other disciplines are supressed by the powers that be, they do not wish new scientific evidence to come to light, which will prove the existence of superior knowledge and supra-scientific modalities, many millennia before our so called scientific Age. Institutions and Universities are pulling out all of the stops, trying to ignore and deny the new paradigm that is now in its birth phase. <u>Students are being lied to en masse</u>!!

What's more, it is very easy to prove this, we find the discoveries of Sam Osmanagich, professor of Anthropology in Bosnia, relating to five gigantic pyramids in that country, continually blocked and repressed in the mainstream media, and by institutions all over Europe. People were even threatened with their jobs, if they go and help Sam dig out ancient tunnels, leading to the main pyramid – which he calls the Pyramid of the Sun. This pyramid, is almost twice the size of the Great Pyramid of the Giza Plateau, and the authorities are blocking him from opening it up. [2017]

The pyramids in question, were covered for untold millennia by earth, trees and other forms of rough terrain; they merely resembled hills to people who lived in the local environment – but now, all that has changed, because of a keen-eyed and astute Bosnian professor.

Measuring angles and viewing these structures from various locations and perspectives, Sam ultimately recognized the 'pyramidal-signature' that all terrestrial pyramids flag, when a genuine pyramid is covered in soil and grass.

He is restricted to digging out tunnels which criss-cross the flat ground between the pyramids in this area – an area very close to the Bosnian town of Visoko.

What is so Important about the Bosnian Pyramids?

The importance lies in the fact that Sam Osmanagich has proved, using current scientific techniques such as Radio Carbon 14 dating, that the tunnels leaning to the main pyramid there, are at least 14.000 years old! The pyramids themselves, he estimates to be around 34.000 years old.

What is probably just as important, he has discovered healing chambers along the route of these tunnels – which still function to this day. One particular chamber produces ultra-sound via a complex interaction of natural forces, impacting through a ceramic megalith, situated on the floor of this chamber. Sam brought in experts in sound, ground penetrating radar, and various subtle energies, to ascertain what is really happening within this chamber.

The ultra-sound produced in this particular chamber, Sam tells us, acts as a cleansing mechanism for human beings – killing bacteria and viruses in the human body. Somehow, the ancients had designed and constructed a healing chamber that does not even exist today – its purpose we can only guess at, but it seems that it served as a cleansing process for people passing further and further along the tunnels, and towards the Great Pyramid of the Sun. It is now obvious that the pyramid structure is a cosmic energy amplification device, which will amplify subtle-energies within its confines. These cosmic energies where harnessed and then utilized by early civilizations to power, and operate unusual modalities now lost to us! Information like this, is routinely supressed by the powers that be, and also in relation to other archaeological sites dotted around the globe. We are on the verge of **a new scientific paradigm** and there is no turning back!

Workers, helping to dig-out the various tunnels in this area, while resting in this chamber, experience respite from various ailments such as arthritis, joint pain, repertory problems, stiffness and other health problems. **This healing-chamber still functions** untold millennia after its initial inception, design and construction – nothing short of a minor miracle!

Sam has single-handedly proved the existence of a superior scientific modality, older than 14.000 years. It is older than this, because the tunnels we filled in by an antique civilization 14.000 years ago, but they were probably not the people who originally built the pyramid and tunnel complex! Added to this, Sam has discovered many other supra-scientific modalities still operating within the pyramid complex – these he has documented in several online videos.

What I am alluding to here, is merely the 'tip of iceberg' – large numbers of new discoveries in Anthropology, Archaeology, Egyptology and Para-history are being systematically supressed; because they do not fit the current scientific paradigm.

This subject of suppression and the hiding of new discoveries from antiquity, is now, for the first time, being discussed openly on the internet, by a raft of new thinkers and intrepid explorers. We find such people as Carmen Boulter and John Anthony West, openly contradicting the orthodox and stifled teachings we find everywhere in our culture today.

Contemporary science and Egyptology continuously remain in abject-ignorance regarding the contruction, and purpose of the Egyptian pyramids. Upon researching this paradigm for 30 years, it is very clear indeed that the scientific community have **no clue,** as to the purpose or the methods of contruction, where these pyramids are concerned.

This single item, of the inconvenient existence of sophisticated sacred structures in Egypt and elsewhere, flags our complete ignorance of this paradigm. <u>In this respect, we are like little children in a game meant for adults</u>!

Orthodox Egyptologists expect us to believe that these colossal mega-structures were designed and build in 20 years, using only copper chisels, hemp-rope and slave-labour. In fact, if we look closely at the Egyptian sites, we can clearly see evidence of machine-tooling on the stones and artefacts! We are being lied to on an industrial scale!

Modern 'science' and archaeology continually cite theories and 'facts' about these structures in Egypt, which have now become so ridiculous and dated, that it is embarrassing to the astute and seasoned listener.

This subject is important, because it shows how on the one hand 'science' and modern 'education' is out of kilter with **what is actually happening in the world today**, and on the other, how certain elements within the establishment and the universities are strongly resisting the investigation of newly discovered archaeological sites, all over the world. This is so, because they cannot be explained by conventional 'science', nor by established historical timelines set down by these same establishments - in ignorance!

We can see clearly from the discoveries of the Bosnian Pyramids, and other facets of long lost civilizations formerly of the Earth, that the scientific paradigm is about to shift in this, the twenty first century. Cracks are already beginning to appear in the conventional theories on para-history and the ancient wisdom possessed by former civilizations on our Earth.

Pioneers such as Sam Osmanagich in Bosnia, and Carmen Boulter in Egypt are forcing a re-think of ideas and theories formerly 'set in concrete'. The old anachronistic theories on para-history, anthropology and archaeology are beginning to look very jaded and absurd, in the face of newly discovered artefacts, temples, sacred structures, and hidden technology. A technology that does not even conform to modern physics - the physics we are taught at school. What paradoxes are now set to confront the fossilized mind-set of contemporary peoples. We are about to be tested by a massive and decisive change in our scientific paradigm. A change that is about to sweep away, old and anachronistic thinking, half-truths and lame-theories that served to fill gaps in our knowledge for too long. <u>Knowledge empowers: Great Knowledge has the power to change one's destiny</u>!

References:

The Pyramid Code: 5 part Documentary Series on the Egyptian Pyramids By Carmen Boulter PhD.

Schooling The World: Insightful Documentary into the Hidden Agendas

Within Contemporary 'Education' Worldwide.

Revelations of the Pyramids: Documentary Exposing Some of the Real

Facts about Pyramids & other Sites around the World.

Pyramids Around the World and What is Happening in the Bosnian Pyramid Tunnels:

Youtube videos on the Bosnian Pyramids and Doctor Sam Osmanagich, unique anthropologist and archaeologist. [Not to be missed!]

Fear And The Herd Mentality

Why is it that more people are not empowered, and especially women? Fear and conformity are the twin elements here, that prevent people from developing their intelligence, freedom and cognitive level.

Many religions, where the covert goals are **control and subservience**, tell their adherents that 'they are the chosen ones': they are special, and are among the few, who will be saved by 'the almighty'.

This, of course, is only the greatest con ever devised by man. It extracts terrified compliance from those subject to this strategy. No one wishes to be 'the one not saved by the almighty': cast out to the outer-darkness for all eternity.

Family

Then there is the item which most people fall for - family. It is necessary to develop one's own intelligence outside of the cocooned world of the family ethos and family protection – one must become independent.

In many cases, conservative families do not like this, and will make every effort to maintain their control over your life, and call the shots. They will often go to extreme measures in certain cases to maintain your compliance. They will lie to you, manipulate you, even threaten you - if it appears that other strategies are not working. But one must never surrender one's integrity and freedom because of threats or comfort - this would be a complete abdication of our primary responsibility to ourselves -

The Con:

Your family is everything, and one must comply with family rules and traditions, if one is to maintain respect and protection from the said family. On occasions, one may be threatened with removal from the family will or inheritance, if we decide to plot our own course in life and become independent of our family, in thought and action.

It is very often the case, that failure to comply will incur penalties and most certainly, various forms of verbal abuse.

Sometimes, complete failure to accept the trite and crass conditions laid down by one's 'tribe', will result in expulsion from the 'tribe': all 'rights' rescinded and one's character trashed.

This is simply a method of keeping you in line - to do their bidding! It has to be said that, many people fall for this gambit and are too fearful and timid to stand up for themselves.

When we examine this paradigm objectively, we soon come to understand that this is a type of slavery - by the back door.

There is nothing more important than one's freedom, dignity and choice. The fearful compliance with the dictates of family through intimidation, or because of religion and tradition, is a form of madness. The same can be said of remaining chained to our family or religion because of comfort or societal convenience.

All freedom, all dignity and all building of real character has a price-tag. Nothing is to be had for free in this domain - one must pay for one's freedom and position in the world. Compliance with the trite and often ill-informed wishes of relatives or friends, is an abdication of our duty to ourselves - to our own soul!

Our first duty is to ourselves, to our own wellbeing and to our health – both physical and psychological. This is a principle which many people overlook!

The Invitation – The Oriah Mountain Dreamer ... Indian Elder

"It doesn't interest me if the story you are telling is true,
I want to know if you can disappoint another to be true to yourself,
If you can hear the accusation of betrayal and not betray your own soul.
I want to know if you can be faithful and therefore trustworthy,
I want to know if you can see beauty, even if it's not pretty every day.
And if you can source your life from God's presence.
I want to know if you can live with failure, yours and mine. And still stand
on the edge of a lake and shout to the silver of the moon - 'Yes'.

So What is Going On?

What is happening, is, people are trading their freedom and autonomy for security and comfort – this is the real truth of the matter.

This security however, is artificial. The moment one ceases to comply with one's family, the husband/wife or parents, one is excluded from that 'security' or comfort. It is a false-economy. We have to see-through this grand illusion! For those who are not constrained by intimidation, comfort, kudos, … convenience and prestige are often the 'honey-trap'. We tend to be very complacent when it comes to our own betterment and freedom – attachment to material things and to people seems to be the order of the day.

Then What Happens?

We find ourselves in a worse position than before - we are often full of fear, apprehension, lacking in self-confidence, self-esteem and life skills. When we use our family as a cocoon against the world, we are very often **not growing and not maturing emotionally.** Ironically, it is being in life and developing skills and qualities to deal with life, that we become tempered with ability, confidence, maturity and deeper aspirations.

The Reality

Expectations and assumptions by family or friends are mere poisons that weigh us down - curtail our freedom, intelligence and ultimately our happiness.

One can love and respect one's family and friends, without allowing ourselves to be dominated or manipulated. Really, it's a no-brainer!

On the other hand, if certain groups, including religious and cult-type groups, are unwilling to relinquish their control over you - you had better watch out! No balanced, sane or spiritually developed person or persons, will wish to control or manipulate others - period! This is a simple fact of life.

Many such people, will, of course, operate through subterfuge and cunning. They will tell you it is for your own good - they know better than you!

This may hold good if you are very young, immature and naive, but if you are over eighteen, mature, intelligent, sensitive and possess a sound sense of reality - it is very possible that you are being manipulated. Bear in mind, that, you may be quite young and still insist on your rights – human rights are an inalienable right of all, not just certain age groups.

Even if you are in your teens or younger, you do possess certain basic human rights which protect your dignity, health and sanity. I suggest if you are in this position, that you get to know your rights, that is, your human rights or civil liberties. **Knowing your civil liberties may preserve your sanity, and maybe even save your life!**

Breaking-Free

Ultimately, breaking-free depends on two definitive qualities - intelligence and inner-maturity. Inner-maturity gives courage and tenacity.

When one sees through the none sense, the lies and contrived advice, one then requires the courage and maturity to break-free!

The best way to do this, is to comprehend totally and without a shadow of a doubt, that you have nothing to lose by taking back your power and taking back your freedom. In reality, in most cases, you have everything to gain in these scenarios.

One must be prepared to 'pay the price', for this leap towards freedom and self-autonomy. It must be undertaken with the attitude - 'whatever happens, there is no turning back: it's all or nothing!'.

Unless one is totally committed to this 'jail-break' - you will fail. Your friends, family, religious companions, cult members, working colleagues etc. know you - that means they also know your weaknesses, your 'soft-spots'.

They will apply pressure to these 'soft-spots', just as soon as you declare your intention to be autonomous.

In some cases, 'all hell will break loose', some people, especially family, feel they have some kind of God-given-right to possess you and direct your life!

It is not so - merely a gambit on their part, to persuade you to put 'your chains' back on. This can also be a husband or wife who has mal-treated you for some time. Don't fall for it! **Grab freedom with both hands.**

Freedom, Knowledge, Wisdom and Intelligence

Freedom and intelligence are 'two sides of a single coin'. Intelligence can only grow in freedom - there is no other way!

We are not accustomed to think like this, because of our strong and all- pervasive societal programming.

Another way of looking at it, is that, bondage and a lack of true freedom retards and blocks the development of intelligence.

Great freedom in life gives a space, a 'launch-pad' for the development of authentic intelligence, character and integrity. **This, of course, if we are able to recognise the opportunity that presents this opening.**

However, one must understand that freedom by itself, is not enough to develop real intelligence in us - it is also a necessity to add knowledge and wisdom to the equation.

Knowledge, and here I am referring to higher knowledge, not academia and science, provides the data for the expansion of our being and our consciousness – wisdom shows us <u>how to make use</u> of this knowledge. It is 'the key that operates the lock'

Different Levels of Freedom

One must understand that there are different levels and layers of freedom and intelligence - some of which are beyond our mortal gaze!

Nevertheless, we can begin with self-empowerment and the struggle for self-autonomy. This is a big aim for most people, and once achieved, it sets the stage for 'the scaling of higher peaks'.

Nothing can be achieved in life, generally speaking, without this self-empowerment and freedom. It is the foundation, the wellspring from which all other achievements manifest.

> *'When people are intimidated by your strength and happiness,*
> *they'll try to tear you down, and break your spirit. Remember,*
> *it's a reflection of their weakness and not a reflection of you.'*

> - Free Spirited. [Internet]

Modern Education - The Illusion of Knowledge and Understanding

Truth creates a great stir; it 'ruffles the feathers of sleepers', those who have never questioned the artificial and contrived system that surrounds them.

Modern 'education' has nothing to do with knowledge, wisdom and real understanding; in fact, it could not be further from authentic living and Truth. Nothing is transmitted which helps one understand oneself, the many problems of life and, the universe which encapsulates us. We are kept in the dark with regards para-history, authentic Egyptology, new discoveries in anthropology and esoteric wisdom is treated as a pariah. We do not develop emotional maturity within our 'education' system; students leaving our sphere of 'education' are very often lacking in communication skills, confidence and self-esteem, a wide world horizon, qualities necessary for a harmonious life .... sensitivity, compassion, tact, courage to follow one's own path in life, insight, fortitude, resourcefulness, foresight, etc.

With the introduction of authentic knowledge comes an understanding of the need to acquire certain qualities and skills in life: not just a capacity to sit behind a computer or build a career. We come to understand how important it is to expand one's capacity and innate nature as a human being. **This particular instruction, is completely absent from modern education.**

For contemporary people, this is a paradox. This is so, because modern people have no conception of authentic knowledge, wisdom and Truth. They simply have no experience of these things - it is outside their remit.

> *"Modern education is a form of imposed ignorance." - Noam Chomsky.*

The more we conform to 'education' and University teachings, the more we become brainwashed. We are duped by the System into believing that our 'education system' is 'gold standard' and 'cutting-edge' - nothing could be further from the Truth. Over the past one hundred years or so, education has been 'dumbed-down' on purpose, and this can be easily verified with a little research, especially in the U.S.A where the power possessors at the time, openly flaunted their intentions in this direction.

"The great purpose of school can be realized better in dark, airless, ugly places ... " "It is to master the physical self ... to transcend the beauty of nature."

"School should develop the power to withdraw from the external world."

-William Torrey Harris. U.S. Commissioner of
Education. 1889 – 1906.

In fact, the basic characteristics and modus operandi of how we educate our young people, and also, adult education has not changed ... they are still taught in sterile environments called class-rooms, or in banal and depressing lecture halls.

We will, no doubt, look back in centuries to come and react with shock and amazement, at how we are currently treating students. How retarded is the mind-set that teaches people in this fashion ... a top-down structure of instruction, from a set of structures and artificial parameters, which even the ancient Greeks would never have accepted.

N.B. Please see the very interesting documentary - 'Schooling the World' by Carol Black - on Youtube. 'A lost peoples film.'

In reality, modern education is a form of social repression just like hyper-taxation and mandatory vaccinations.

We currently have a powerful system of repression in place, one which is cunning and covert, and operates beneath the dull perceptions of 'the collective radar'.

There are many strata of awareness connected to freedom and intelligence, one of which is certainly **to see through the dark shadow of repression,** for what it really is - a system which the ignorant and naive mistake for freedom!

Should we wish to develop further, to levels that transcend self-empowerment, freedom and expanded terrestrial intelligence, we must explore the esoteric world of higher knowledge and arcane wisdom. A sphere the collective considers impossible and unreal; because of societal conditioning and a diminished cognitive level.

Nonetheless, it exists, and for the wise and intrepid, it is the final destination for all intelligent mortal souls, willing to risk, living a life contrary to jaded and outmoded traditions, and seeking self-mastery at the highest levels.

The collective are asleep, dreaming that they are awake - slaves believing they are free. Gurdjieff came to show us a different reality - a different Path; to point the way to new possibilities, new horizons - with him, he brought an ancient wisdom, forgotten in the mists of time. He also issued a warning that the Earth was currently in a dangerous phase of its existence, and was not guaranteed to survive the black-alchemy en-vogue, in this, the Kali-Yuga Cycle of Earth's existence … the Age of iron, steel, gadgets and lies.

A global war cannot be discounted, from which mankind cannot survive. This is a very real possibility in this Age – a war with nuclear weapons and newly developed modalities, so wicked, that we will scarce believe our eyes when they are used. Modern technology has been side-tracked into the service of creating weapons, so evil, that many of them are not openly spoken of.

Intelligence dictates that we must move away from such dark modalities; into a new paradigm of knowledge, light, compassion, love and deep understanding and if we cannot do this as a collective, we must do it at an individual level. The challenge remains for each one of us dedicated to knowledge and authentic living, to build around us the components of a higher way of live. Difficult thought this may be, it is not impossible by any means – the knowledge and profound wisdom that will make this a reality is not lost or completely hidden, we are just too asleep to recognise it, and use it!

> *"This work is beautiful because when you see why it exists and what it means, it is about liberation. It is as beautiful as if, locked for years in a prison, you see a stranger entering who offers you a key. But you refuse it because you have acquired prison-habits and have forgotten your origin - which is from the stars!"*

> - Maurice Nicoll.

Our potential as human beings is awesome, and beyond the average person's ability to conceive of - we are operating at about one tenth of our potential; even as ordinary people. However, without the conscious efforts to develop certain rudimentary qualities, abilities and aptitudes in ourselves, we remain largely static.

I say conscious efforts, because if we leave everything to our culture, and our upbringing, we are largely in the dark with regards how to develop inner-power in ourselves and in others. Conscious efforts entails going beyond culture-bound-reason, narrow-educational-modalities, and artificial family attitudes and requirements. We **are not bound by these things**, they have power over us only if we accept their authority and autonomy over our lives - we have the choice to take them or leave them. This is the key element which needs to be understood – there is always a choice, and breaking away from mini-dictators entails a price – nothing worthwhile on this Earth comes free.

When we decide to leave them, it means to a degree, going beyond social convention and living contrary to narrow and banal societal mores. **Freedom is just around the corner.**

Our lives are not set in stone, we can choose to walk the path less chosen; our destiny can alter with the introduction of Great Wisdom and knowledge!

"Great Knowledge changes destiny." - Ancient Chinese Proverb.

Making A Decision to Liberate Oneself

It is said, in the annals of esoteric teachings, that the decision to liberate oneself is more difficult to come to, that the process itself.

Making the decision, one has to contend with a host of ingrained mental and emotional habits, together with pressures from family, friends and perhaps even our spouse?

The Reality Is

Hidden behind social convention and banal cultural rules, is the fact that **we have nothing to lose!** In reality, our fears, apprehensions, anxieties, and doubts are artificial - they are mostly culturally generated.

There is nothing in this world quite like liberating oneself from fake cultural mores and artificial belief-systems.

"The art of knowing is knowing what to ignore." -Rumi.

In the end it comes down to courage; without courage we will remain in our usual mind-set: not questioning the structure or ethos of our surroundings. This is a mistake on a vast scale, but we are conditioned by society to accept our lot and not to question the status quo.

"When your education limits your imagination, it's called indoctrination."

-Nicola Tesla.

We do not have the power nor the time to change others, or to change society, but we do have the innate power to change ourselves. Incrementally, and over time, we can **become a better version of who we are right now.**

Liberation for Women

When we expand our cognitive ability beyond that of the average person on the street, we begin to perceive things around us, which formerly stood outside our cognitive-radar.

We begin to see how badly women are treated in our societies today [2017]; how they are subtly marginalized and treated by many men as 'lesser-mortals'.

This is a sad state of affairs, since women are deserving of so much more; in fact, deserving of great reverence and respect.

Women put up with so much nonsense from men, gender bias, sarcasm and even downright hostility on occasions. Should one do serious research on these issues, it is impossible not to be shocked – women are constantly undermined by a social structure geared towards men and the masculine principle!

In Ancient Times:

We find, with some research, that women were actually treated much better within certain ancient cultures on the Earth.

In ancient Egypt for example, we find women were not only held in high regard but revered as representations of the Goddess. It was understood at that time, that the feminine principle had a very important role to play in life: a woman was an earthly manifestation of the divine feminine principle – without which no harmony could be attained in life.

Kindness, sensitivity, supportiveness, healing, nurturing, compassion, natural healing and herbal-medicine, are required to balance the masculine qualities of leadership, tenacity, courage, confidence, fire and action.

Ref: 'The Pyramid Code' by Carmen Boulter.

Five Part Documentary on the Myths and Half-Truths Surrounding Pyramids.

Thus, back then, women had a higher status in many ancient cultures, they could divorce easily, own land, even become a pharaoh in the land of Kent … Egypt, as did Hatchet soot …. one of the few female pharaohs in dynastic Egypt.

What is Really Happening with Women Today?

The reality Is, women have no idea how to marshal their own innate powers – this is a conundrum for most contemporary women. Actions and decisions should not be based on material gains from a person or a situation, but what one accomplishes spiritually and internally, in terms of wisdom and happiness! Materiality does not give happiness – this is merely an illusion which soon fades to reveal a deep-seated emptiness inside.

A Three Step Process:
1. A woman must realize for herself that she needs to do certain spiritual- work, to balance and integrate herself.
2. She must do this all important work, without procrastination.
3. She then must learn how to collect her energies and how to project them. This knowledge cannot be obtained in our ordinary profane society, it belongs to esoteric wisdom and a time when women were properly understood and respected.

Women are conditioned from very young, via societal programming, to conform to feminine stereotypes; behaving within strict and highly limiting parameters. A woman has to become aware of this, and she has to understand how to combat it, without becoming aggressive, manipulative, controlling or vengeful. She must learn how to collect her force, with calm, intelligence and precision – not wasting her force on trivia, micro-politics and banal disputes with others. The correct projection of one's force is critical here!

A woman's conditioning is insidious; it is very often disputed by contemporary psychologists, but nonetheless exists. Young women are subtly taught via societal influences in the media and elsewhere, that looking good is what a woman must aspire to at all times. Underweight women are paraded on the fashion cat-walks around the world, and herded backstage like so many cattle.

'Looking good' is seen as a 'ticket' to success, a career, marriage, and every opportunity that presents itself in life.

This covert training of young women's psychology, creates a wrong focus on appearances and externals. Women in many respects, see themselves as an addendum or adjunct to men; as subservient, and with subsequent consequences of poor confidence and low self-esteem.

This scenario is strongly reinforced via societal media, and via our misguided 'educational' system.

The problem being that women buy into all of this, and never question the status quo. The lure is to be attractive and acquire power over men – which of course, is merely external power and not inner-power, for some potential opportunity perhaps, to a higher lifestyle. This is the pay-off.

Many women feel powerless in contemporary societies, so they grab any form of power to hand; this is a type of abdication of integrity and authentic inner-power – we cannot grow spiritually by merely relying on personal appearances.

Low Confidence and Self-Esteem

Today, there is a widespread culture of low confidence and self-esteem among women, and here I am particularly referring to the U.K. I can vouch for this personally, since it became obvious to me during my years as a holistic counsellor and therapist. [Most of my clientele were women]

This singular phenomenon demonstrates how detrimental 'the system' is for women – they are robbed of many natural innate qualities and abilities – so important for the harmonic maturation and emotional development of their gender. Women are not aware of what has happened to them, they do not comprehend that they have been conditioned and programmed simply by being a part of a sterile and inept system, many feel lost and depressed – not knowing how to approach this conundrum. Many women are medicated, simply because they are unable to express their natural abilities and essential nature in contemporary society – they become imbalanced and desperate. This is the great irony of modern times – women are marginalized in such a subtle and insidious way.

Many people dispute this, even some women, and many so called 'experts' – but unless one has an expanded cognitive ability, one cannot see this phenomenon for what it is!

So ingrained is this situation, that young women grow up into adulthood very often without genuine confidence and self-esteem; not realizing what is at the root of their problems. I have had a steady stream of wonderful ladies come to my counselling sessions, and at the root of many of the presenting problems we find the bête-noir – low confidence and self-esteem.

When young ones are home schooled, with a combination of parents and private tutors, we find this situation is very often reversed.

However, since so many women are brainwashed, they just accept their lot, and never question the ethos or structure of their society.

An Advanced Culture

In an advanced culture, that is, an advanced spiritual culture, women would not be subject to such contrived indoctrination – they would experience a freedom difficult to describe.

They would be accorded a freedom and respect befitting their refined nature. Women today, are incredibly undervalued and undermined – we see this all around us in almost every society. We find them lost and isolated in very many cases – a subtle and hidden crime against all womanhood.

With a correct understanding and valuation of the feminine principle, they would not be treated as a type of second class citizen, nor would they have to suffer in silence; women could reclaim their power!

Women Taking Back Their Power

From the esoteric perspective, it is essential that a person does not give away their power to others, or to institutes – as we see happening all the time within contemporary cultures. We give our power away every time we vote, every time we send our children to schools to be indoctrinated by a crass system of mind-control. We give our power away when we enrol for a college or University course, having outdated theories and history piled on us. We give our power away when we go to our doctors and accept medication without doing our own research on our condition, and on the side-effects of that particular medication.

This applies even more so to women – who are basically repressed in our contemporary cultures. The trick is not so much in the actual repression, but in the cunning mechanism of getting women to accept it as **normal**. Men, are also in need of lessons in taking back their power – from their situation, although somewhat different, they require a definitive adjustment to banal societal forces!

A Woman's Lot:

Women, in fact, put up with so much none sense from men, and sometimes other women, it is quite unreal. <u>Many women think all of this is normal</u>.

Large numbers give their power away to bullies, lovers, religious figures, gurus, politicians, and partners – without even realizing it!

It is often done on a subtle level; people give their power away en-masse to governments, politicians and the medical establishment. It is, of course, not viewed in this way by the majority of people – when it comes to 'seeing the writing on the wall', most people are completely brainwashed.

> *'As long as you remain within that field of the culture, of society, of greed, of envy, of achievement, you are not a free human being. You may think that you have free-will, but you are just a part of the monstrous society, a conditioned human being.'*
>
> *-J. Krishnamurti.*

The Non-Static Paradigm and Man's Stupidity

When we look at things objectively, we can clearly see our own stupidity. We cannot look at life from a static paradigm, because it is steadily moving forward and evolving, after a certain fashion. We do not take this into account in our calculations of life and living.

Life is a continuous stream; it is never static – in this light, we can see how ridiculous it is, to take things existing today, here and now, as the ultimate way or achievement. Yet, we act and behave as though everything is 'locked in concrete'.

In three or four hundred years from now, if our planet survives man's hubris and violent & oppressive ways, we will look back in horror at how children were 'educated', how we ignorantly consumed mountains of pharmaceutical medicines – which often do more harm than good, how people followed blindly, religious dogma, and how, political systems, often antiquated and unchanged for hundreds of years, maintained a grip on millions of people worldwide – even though, at the time, they could clearly be seen to be failing.

We collectively fail to understand how primitive our world currently is – advances in 'science' and technology have brought us **the illusion** of progress. But the real marker of our progress and development as a civilization, is war. In a superior culture there can be no war – this is an objective litmus test.

The key element here, of course, is that we fail to question anything! We never question the ethos or structure of our surroundings – we behave like non-intelligent beings in a Universe alive with mystery and profound knowledge in the background. We accept the banal and repressive societal mechanisms and dictates - over adventure, freedom and wisdom! **Then we wonder why we suffer?**

Somehow, we put up with this omnipresent suffering because we see it as a price we must pay for what we receive in our culture. This is, of course, not so! The train of action and reaction does not work like this. We suffer because of the abject loss of thinking for ourselves – **we do not think for ourselves.** Our acceptance of the status quo puts us in a unique disposition – we are poisoned by contemporary medicines, duped by politicians, lied to by omission by doctors, brainwashed via our 'education system', given false knowledge by our Universities and colleges on the key subjects of Anthropology, Archaeology, Egyptology, para-history, psychology, and sociology.

We cannot change the external world – this is a fact, it progresses at its own pace over vast spans of time, but we can certainly change our inner-world through self-empowerment to begin with, and later the acquisition of higher wisdom.

The great secret lies in the word **wisdom**, for it is the ancient esoteric wisdom of the Earth, paradoxically, that our future depends.

As individuals, we can improve our life dramatically by the exploration and adoption of these truly great ancient ideas and teachings. This profound avenue is open to us, but it is first necessary to perceive its existence, and secondly to have a correct evaluation of its great power and integrity.

> *"Without self-knowledge, without understanding the workings and functions of his machine, man cannot be free, he cannot govern himself and he will always remain a slave."*

> -G.I. Gurdjieff.

In this manual, I cover many issues that touch upon the whole gamut of inner-power and self-development. There are many hints and tips included, together with sections on relationships, confidence & self-esteem, finding one's gifts, adaptability, patterns in our lives, finding our inner-weaknesses and correcting them, ancient wisdom and more. I suggest that the reader, if not acquainted with this type of knowledge and modality, pursue a course of study into the future, this, presuming you have a genuine interest in the subject. You will find out in due course, that it is much more than a subject, but encompasses all and everything that is truly authentic and profound on this Earth!

Esoteric teachings have been filtered out of the race-consciousness with great success and deviousness: take back your power and re-possess that which is fundamentally your birth right – brainwashing is very much reverseable!!

Section 1

The Chakras: A brief overview of the 'chakras' or centres in Man from the perspective of Esoteric Psychology

The Seven Chakras or Centres in Terrestrial Beings

In every human being there exists a physical body and a counter part or energy body, this is sometimes called the Aura or Body of Light. It has seven centres of power existing in its make-up and many sub-centres throughout its structure. These energy centres or 'chakras' are of vital importance to us in the field of esoteric study, since it is from these energy centres that all real power is determined in the human bio-machine.

When we deal with the inner-development of man, we are in reality dealing with the development (or non-development) of these subtle energy centres.

These energy centres in the make-up of a terrestrial being have independent mechanisms, intelligence, vibratory levels, energy and also many subtle but vital functions to perform; both in the physical body and in the spiritual elements of an individual.

The Seven Centres in Terrestrials Are:

1. Moving Centre;
2. Instinctive Centre;
3. Sex Centre;
4. Intellectual Centre;
5. Emotional Centre;
6. Higher Intellectual Centre; and
7. Higher Emotional Centre.

It must be stressed:

The knowledge which we are in the process of unfolding here, comes from esoteric schools and <u>can not be found</u> among our ordinary social inventions or theories on life.

The two higher centres [at 6 & 7 above] are extremely special in that, in most <u>normal</u> terrestrial peoples, they ARE FUNCTIONING <u>but remain unconnected to the other five centres </u>which operate during the normal functioning of our organism in our everyday lives.

What must be understood is <u>that</u> we do not just have one mind but in fact <u>many minds</u>! The belief that we have just one mind is an error or flaw in how we think and how we see things.

The chakra system in humans has, in fact, been alluded to in many of the ancient and also current incomplete systems of knowledge. These include the Hindu, Buddhist and Tantric materials; but a complete and authentic overview of the chakras has never been expounded to Mankind in general.

Each centre represents a different major brain function in human beings and is quite independent from the other centres in many respects. In order to learn about our inner-world, it is first necessary to learn about the chakras or centres. <u>Central to the esoteric teaching on the energy centres is that they do not function properly; they often steal energy from one another and one centre often takes over the role and function of another centre!</u>

1. Moving Centre

This centre controls movement in the body and such things as our physical activity, watching television etc. When for instance, one learns a new skill for the first time, let us say driving a car, the mind centre or intellectual centre will struggle with this challenge primarily and then, once mastered, it passes the complete 'mechanism' for driving into the moving centre for future recall. (It then becomes automatic and without a direct involvement of the mind).

One of the biggest problems seems to be with people differentiating between moving-centre functions and instinctive-centre functions. The main difference being as follows: our instinctive-centre functions are inborn ... such as digestion, heartbeat and our immune system etc.;

whereas our moving-centre functions or manifestations <u>have to be learned</u>. Moving centre also controls such things as dreams in our nightly sleep and our daytime dreams or our 'day-dreaming'.

2. Instinctive Centre

This brain function controls all of our instinctive functions, such as instinctive fear, instinctive movements and instinctive reactions to many situations, people or often even places. This includes our so called inner 'hunches', the functioning of our organs, breathing and circulation of the blood.

3. Sex Centre

This brain function controls our sexual drive, our passion or lack of it. Our sex centre works on very fine energy; much finer than that of, say, our moving centre or intellectual centre. This centre, too, is different from the others in that it does not possess positive or negative halves. Thus, there is no such thing as negative sex.

4. Intellectual Centre

The intellectual centre controls our thoughts and our reasoning. Our centres will sometimes swap their functions for that of another; for instance, thinking centre will take over for emotional centre and vice versa. Moving centre will often step in for intellectual centre for a time and so on. This swapping of functions can, if it is maintained on a prolonged basis, render the person imbalanced or, what modern psychology terms neurotic or dysfunctional.

Under certain specific circumstances, when for instance one is reading and also simultaneously preoccupied with something else, moving centre will take over the function of reading in a mechanical fashion. Where, for instance, we are vocally reading aloud, we will continue to do so, as before, but in a crude and mechanical way, our tone of voice being audibly different.

5. Emotional Centre

This particular brain function controls our feelings. Our feelings work with a strong and very explosive energy, many times more refined than our mental centre.

Under ordinary conditions of life, we have <u>no control</u> over our emotional-centre or instinctive centre and we have only very little control over our moving centre. For example, <u>we cannot</u> be angry or glad without cause and this cause <u>is usually</u> an external one. In other words, our emotional and instinctive centres are controlled mainly from without; by external stimuli.

N.B.

Our <u>negative emotions</u> originate in the emotional centre; but this centre does not have a negative aspect to it <u>as ordained by Nature</u>. Strictly speaking, it is formed by 'an artificial graft' attached to the emotional centre from early childhood. To express negative emotions means to loose vast amounts of our precious psychic energy!

6 & 7 Higher Emotional & Higher Intellectual Centres

These centres are fully functional in all normal people but <u>are not connected</u> to the functioning of the lower chakras. This by analogy is rather like a huge power plant fully operational and functioning but not hooked-up to the power grid. This means that, in each normal human being, the potential exists for a powerful alliance between the incredibly powerful higher centres and the five lower ones.

The two higher centres, unlike the lower centres previously described, possess a vast psychic potential for higher-consciousness in humans. They are both functioning in perfectly <u>normal human beings</u> but remain 'disconnected' in all unregenerate terrestrials. The problem is that <u>our lower centres are undeveloped and also not functioning as they should</u> in order to facilitate such a connection. Before such a connection can be made, the lower centres require 'adjusting and cleansing' in a specific way; otherwise, a premature *amalgam of forces* would prove disastrous!

The idea relating to the seven chakras in human beings is very old; in fact it comes from remote antiquity; from esoteric schools before the dawn of history. It must be understood that the division of our brain into seven definitive centres or functions cannot be discovered in any ordinary way.

When we are instructed with regard to the division of centres in human beings, we may even observe them in ourselves with some difficulty and find that this division is true; the reality is, ordinary mind cannot discover their existence unaided or by itself – nor by research!

It must further be understood that each of the five lower energy centres, with the exception of the sex centre, is divided into three parts: higher, middle and lower. This higher part of a centre represents the highest intelligence of that particular centre; the middle part represents its dynamic energy; and the lower represents its mechanical part, its formative function.

Inner-power comes from accessing the higher parts of our energy centres; this feat requires effort on our part; attention and self-observation. Another way of looking at it, is that, deep pondering on our situation, qualities and our life requires us to use the higher parts of centres and, most importantly, more than one centre. We are required to go beyond ourselves, our often narrow and self-centred agenda, our small repertoire of thoughts and limited parameters of awareness and knowledge.

From the general perspective, most people in society only use the lower parts of centres. Why is this? It is like this because it requires no effort to do so, no attention and less focus. Generally speaking, people are lazy.

> 'A person lives in his or her very small cosmos which is his or her world and this very small world is governed mainly by self-interests. People do not yet even live in this World – this small planet called Earth. This is due to the lack of development of consciousness, as are also so many of the troubles of this Earth. Consciousness, in the majority of people, is confined to the very small world of themselves and their own interests. We have scarcely any proper consciousness of one another. We only take in what we are interested in and if a person is only interested in himself and those belonging to his own self-interests, everything said about the Cosmos has little or no meaning, for it demands a form of thinking beyond oneself. A person is glued to his life – thus, he has, as a rule, very little free force in him to think beyond his immediate life-interests.
>
> -Maurice Nicoll.

Tips For Working On Your Energy Centres

- Look at a person's spirit rather than their external form.
- Take up the practice of Chi-Gung or Tai-Chi.
- Visualization work may be added – joins mind & emotional centres.
- Practice empathy & forbearance with others.
- Physical work or exercise also good at clearing centres.
- Sauna & steam very good for lymphatic system and, by reflex, the energy centres.
- Relaxation techniques.
- Stop smoking.
- Stop taking alcohol or drugs.
- Learn new skills.
- Avoid continuous stress.
- Regular and safe sun exposure is very important.
  (Energy from the Sun charges the chakras like a dynamo).

Notes

Section 2

Esoteric Psychology – Man's True Inner Psychology

In order to change one's inner-Being, it is first necessary to know <u>the true structure of Man's inner psychology</u>. This cannot be found in the annals of modern psychology, lectures or books. However, it does form part of the ancient teachings of the Earth and is passed down to us through time, in the form of esoteric teachings.

To understand Man's true inner-psychology requires a new approach to an old problem: we need to change our thinking, our mode of perception. It also requires 'thinking outside the box'; a new valuation.

If we remain rooted in logic and within the limits of our culture-bound mentation, we cannot approach the new concepts esotericism provides us with. From esotericism comes a whole new paradigm of thinking, a vast new world horizon and one which will take us into 'uncharted territory'.

When we are born, we come into being with pure Essence internally; there is nothing of the external world there yet … everything is our own and natural. But, to survive in a complex and sometimes dangerous world, we must develop Personality. However, only Essence can evolve.

Personality allows us to cope with an ever changing array of circumstances around us in ordinary life. Personality, however, surrounds Essence, just like the shell of a nut surrounds the nut. Personality is limited in its evolution because it constitutes only one or two centres (chakras) in man; and in order to develop spiritually, all seven centres must develop in unison.

In addition to these two pivotal elements in man's Being (Essence and Personality), there is a third element: that of the false-ego or superficial-self.

The False-Ego forms part of an individual's personality, but it is completely false, superficial and subsists on fantasy and lies. In many modern people, the False-Ego is very well defined. This pernicious and poisonous element of a person's personality prevents one from seeing oneself and gives us a very wrong picture of what we are. It blocks all authentic human development.

It requires a very specific training to separate from this artificial element in our make up.

The Admixture of Elements in a Man's Being

It must be understood that, in the average person on the street, these three elements are mixed in a person's Being and manifestations; they are not differentiated. In order for a person to develop internally, or spiritually, it is first necessary to separate from this false-ego; and then, work to make Personality passive, while rendering Essence active. This is a definitive process and requires time and effort to achieve.

It is only the ancient teachings of esotericism which show us the way and gives us the means of doing so.

> *'A man must understand certain things. He has thousands of false conceptions, chiefly about himself and he must get rid of some of them before beginning to acquire anything new'*

> **G.I. Gurdjieff.** *(4)*

Essence, Personality and the False-Ego

Firstly, it must be understood that one cannot find this Knowledge being used commonly in contemporary society … it does not exist there. Modern psychology, said Gurdjieff, 'is childish'. It is necessary to have a thirst for Truth; for real meaning in life. *Real meaning* does not exist in ordinary life; ordinary life *cannot be explained in terms of itself.* It can only be explained, and real meaning found, if life is explained from a higher perspective; from Knowledge outside of life … one has to be able to 'stand outside' and 'look back at life'.

Esoteric knowledge is our legacy. It has been handed down to those of us 'who have eyes to see' and 'ears to hear'. People, however, do not see this wisdom nor do they want a share of it in general. They pass over it, not understanding or perceiving its value.

It is necessary to have what one might call *'a healthy dissatisfaction with life and what it has to offer'* before one can truly appreciate this wisdom!

A person who wishes to develop spiritually and truly grow internally must find a way to develop essence. The development of essence and the rendering of personality passive are paramount.

However, to do this requires a whole new approach to life, to one's psychology, to other people and to one's aspirations. To change one's inner-Being requires a higher order of knowledge. Essence cannot change by itself; nor can essence change or grow through one's social environment and the circumstances of ordinary life!

The truth about essence is that it stops growing in the average person at around six or eight years old. Then, personality begins to grow and takes its place, as it were. In rare individuals, essence grows in tandem with a person's chronological age. This may mean that this person is spiritually mature; but this is not always guaranteed. The best combination in the individual, in relation to inner development, is an equal development of essence and personality. This provides the best basis for further work.

> *'Now Essence ceases to grow because it has not the right food from life to grow by. Life can provide the food for the development of personality but not the food necessary for the development of Essence. <u>The secret is that Personality and Essence need different foods for their respective development</u>. They need different kinds of truths. For example, the education of Personality is developed by knowledge of science, but the Essence is not developed by knowing truths of this kind. Essence, before it is manifested in the human body, derived from parents on Earth, comes from a much higher level than the Planetary World; it comes from the solar-sphere of intelligence, under 24 orders of laws ... it has a very high origin ... by comparison, Personality has a very low origin in the cosmic scale. .... But if a man, imbued with the knowledge of esotericism, continually steeps his mind in its Truths and thinks and thinks again from them and perceives*

*their depth, and acknowledges them and applies them to his
inner states, Essence will begin to grow.'*

Maurice Nicoll. *(5)*

In order to understand Essence and Personality better, I have listed
below 'actions from Essence' and 'actions from Personality'. Actions from
Essence always emanate from a deeper and more real part of ourselves.

Personality: Seeking fame.
Essence: Helping others.

Personality: Cold logic.
Essence: Intuition / creativity.

Personality: Grudges.
Essence: Forgiveness.

Personality: Weighing & measuring always.
Essence: Generosity.

Personality: Being cynical.
Essence: Awe & wonderment.

Personality: 'The answer lies in outer-space.'
Essence: 'The answer lies in inner-space.'

Personality: The more friends I have; the better I feel.
Essence: One true friend is worth 20 'fair weather' friends.

Personality: I want to heal my cold!
Essence: I want to heal my life.

Personality: Lack of confidence; bravado.
Essence: Confidence from within.

Personality: I want to educate myself.
Essence: I want to develop myself.

Personality: I want to change the World!
Essence: I want to change myself.

Personality: Science will eventually solve all of our problems.
Essence: Science has probably created as many problems as it has solved.

Personality: With fame & fortune I will achieve great freedom.
Essence: True freedom comes from the death of the False-Ego.

Personality: I love life.
Essence: Life is a clever illusion.

Personality: The answers are out there!
Essence: It is the questions we have wrong!

Personality: 'I already know all of this!'
Essence: 'We really know and understand so little!'

Personality: Superficial life questions.
Essence: Deep pondering and contemplation of life.

Personality: ' … in any case, I will reincarnate and try again later!'
Essence: 'Life is not a dress rehearsal!'

Personality: I need to check with my friends before I decide.
Essence: I need to go deep within myself to my 'inner-compass'.

Personality: I seek knowledge to better my life and get a new job.
Essence: I seek wisdom to enlarge my vision and develop my spirit.

Personality: I am the centre of my Universe.

Essence: Conditioning distorts my vision of life.

Personality: I have learned so much at school today.

Essence: Modern education is a form of imposed ignorance.

Personality: Lord, give me wealth, prosperity & happiness.

Essence: I wish only Wisdom, sincerity & humility.

'Personality developed according to your centre of gravity, will mislead and not give you the force and meaning that you are seeking for. It will not give substance and meaning for your life.'

Maurice Nicoll. *(6)*

Living in personality, one will always be superficial; despite one's best efforts to the contrary; <u>only living in Essence makes life *real*</u>. All efforts in esotericism are first directed towards this end!

With work on Essence comes eventually a new consciousness, sometimes called Real 'I' or the 'Witnessing Consciousness' – this is the aim of all true religions, all Great Schools of thought; all truly Great Paths! We can not get to a higher level of consciousness and inner development, save by this doorway of Essence. Essence is the bridge between personality, or where we are now, and real spiritual growth.

While living in Personality, people are divided, smug and self-obsessed and do not notice this. Personality tends to be judgmental and negative. Living in Essence brings humility, great awareness and compassion. In fact, Essence is the doorway to higher consciousness and to conscience.

It is important that we distinguish in ourselves the difference between the manifestations of Personality and our Essence.

Actions from Personality & Actions from Essence:

Personality always acts in its own selfish interests and, as such, actions from Personality always carry a distinct 'aroma' or 'signature'.

Actions from Personality

- Greedy actions.
- Actions always mechanical & superficial.
- 'Big picture' never taken into account.
- No conscience involved.
- Personality lies continuously.
- Personality manipulates.
- Personality likes 'to be seen of men'.
- Self-justifies.
- Blame.
- Double-standards.

Actions from Essence

- Actions from Essence are holistic in nature.
- Compassion involved.
- Understanding involved.
- Actions from Essence come from a deeper part of Man's Being.
- Unselfish.
- Balanced.
- Simplicity.
- Consideration for others.

The False-Ego

False-personality or the false-ego represents a 'negative core' which is nowadays very commonly formed within personality.

It is <u>not a natural construct</u> in man but is formed in personality due to the artificial and negative influences surrounding an individual in society. It can be viewed as 'the Saboteur' in one's personality, the element in our personality which has the most detrimental effect on our life.

The False-Ego has certain well-defined characteristics and I have listed some of the more prominent traits below for convenience:

- False picture of oneself.
- Imaginary traits and abilities we think we possess.

- False pride.
- Conceit.
- Lacking adaptive thinking.
- Narrow self-interest agenda.
- Great difficulty in forgiving and holds grudges for a long time.
- Lack of humility.
- Absence of Conscience and real sincerity.
- The false-ego always has to be right.
- Finds it difficult to entertain criticism.
- Full of self-importance.
- Overt lack of consideration for others.
- Rigidity of purpose.

Many people are 'held-hostage' by the False-Ego and are unable to manifest themselves directly from their Essence. In many ways, this is a tragedy of huge proportions, since it ruins many human relations which would otherwise be natural and functional.

> *'Hatred paralyzes life;*
> *Love releases it.*
> *Hatred confuses life;*
> *Love harmonizes it,*
> *Hatred darkens life;*
> *Love illuminates it.*

Martin Luther King Jr. (7)

As mentioned above, the false-ego creates many problems in our human relations; creates distress and distrust where none should exist; and brings tension and arrogance to bear on situations where it is not at all necessary. Should one observe people closely and bring into focus tense or negative situations, it is possible to observe the false-ego in action. It always leaves its particular 'tell-tale' signs behind.

In the beginning, it is easier to see this phenomenon in others than in oneself. It is however important to observe it and understand where it emanates from and how it manifests.

Lying forms a cardinal aspect of the nature and modus operandi of the false-ego … it continuously lies, both consciously and unconsciously to protect its own stance and its lack of integrity. It lies to smooth-over its double-standards and lack of charity; its hatred and racial-prejudice.

Next comes the paradigm of learning; all learning by the false-ego is decidedly shallow and one-dimensional. It is always geared towards narrow self-interest and egoism of some form or other.

> *'The ability to learn is not present in all people. A person must learn how to learn anew! A person must not presume that they know or that they can learn anything the please – man is attached to the unreal – he must cultivate an attachment to the real!'*

> -Idries Shah.
> [Learning how to learn] [8]

Tips For Working On Our Inner-Psychology

- Distinguish actions from Personality from that of Essence, in oneself.
- Take regular time out for silence or meditation.
- Seek opportunities to help others and develop empathy.
- Always remember the four powers of Essence: Courage, Sincerity, Humility and Tenacity.
- Practice love, on animals first; they are more receptive.
- Get to know your false-ego; begin by seeing its actions in you!
- Eliminate wrong habits and learn to say sorry when you make a mistake.
- Never seek to profit through the abject loss of another.
- Develop the love of Knowledge – Ancient Wisdom.
- Work on developing patience in oneself.
- Practice forgiveness.

Notes

Section 3

Filters in Man's Psyche

A critical element in the study of esoteric psychology is Man's subtle conditioning and programming in mundane life.

Our modern conditioning of trends, mind-sets, fashions, advertising, parental influences, school programming etc., creates filters in the psyche of today's people. These filters play a much bigger role in our lives than one might suspect; the filters present in the psyche of modern man stop him from perceiving Truth.

In general, modern man is unaware of his potentialities or the Knowledge and efforts required by Great Nature for one to manifest those potentials.

The situation has now arisen that, should an individual decide to seek out Truth, it is first necessary to receive a special preparation in order to facilitate this end. It is no longer possible for a man or a woman to 'enter into' Truth just by merely wishing it; a person must develop a whole new range of understanding, qualities and abilities before this can even begin to happen. A transition period must elapse, wherein a person is prepared, in advance, to receive Truth!

Such is the strength of *the hypnotism of ordinary life.* Because of this strange predicament in the psyche of modern Man, a person now values those elements from life which are unimportant and neglects those rare elements which could give him *something real.*

> *'Be aware, that the science which provides the bridge between the inner and outer life of an individual, is rare, and is transmitted only to those who have been prepared beforehand.*

*'It always happens, that there will be many who will prefer
to accept imitation in place of reality; the superficial in place
of true wisdom!'*

*Hadrat Muinudin Chisti,
Founder of the Chisti Sufi Order. (9)*

The Opposition of Forces

The forces in Nature opposed to our quest are vast <u>and we are only
very small by comparison</u>. We do not fully appreciate the extent of Nature's
power over us and how our everyday lives are affected.

For instance, the very structure of society and how people think
generally flows contrary to all esoteric thought and ways! Society opposes
all true esoteric modes and practices: we are actually dealing with two
opposing forces. On the other hand, esoteric work does not oppose the
mainstream of society or social habit but, rather, makes use of it along the
way, as an athlete will make use of a gym.

Most striking of all is society's ignorance and fear of esoteric
principles and modes of operating. There is also a strange type of
jealousy and negative reaction from various religions etc., which have
fossilized over the centuries and lost the keys to their original knowledge
and wisdom.

There are also definitive cosmic forces which surround us on all sides
and are a permanent feature of our lives on this planet Earth. These all-
powerful cosmic forces are mechanical in nature and are designed to
maintain balance and harmony within the confines of our immediate
cosmos; the Solar System, and beyond. This is their primary function and
role; however, they create, by secondary cause and effect, a World which
has many artificial boundaries for terrestrials; wherein a situation arises as
a result, we must avail ourselves of a Higher Order of Knowledge in order
to escape this 'cosmic restraint'.

*'There is no coming to consciousness without pain.
People will do anything no matter how absurd, in*

order to avoid their own Soul. One does not become enlightened by imagining figures of light, but by making the darkness conscious.'

Carl G. Jung. *(10)*

Tips For Changing Our Social Programming

- EFT. [Emotional Freedom Technique or 'Tapping']
- The Spiritual Autopsy. [Examining one's past up to the present]
- Karma Yoga.
- Spiritual Retreats.
- Spiritual Journeys.
- Practice 'External Considering'. [Consideration of other people.]
- Spiritual Life Coaching.
- Mirror Meditation.
- Tantra.
- Boundary Tapping.
- Literature – 'Feel the Fear and Do It Anyway'.
- Survival Training.
- The Study of Authentic Esoteric Materials – such as G.I Gurdjieff & P.D. Ouspensky.

Notes

Section 4

Addressing Personal Deficiencies

It is important to look at personal deficiencies and how they affect our lives before going into models of repairing them. These have to be faced full-on without blame, judgement or any kind of shame.

We then have to expose some of these weaknesses, contemplate their true significance and recognize those which apply to us personally. There may be some which are not listed here but are important for us to accept as a vital reminder of the work which we have to do!

No one is judged; this work is common to all modern peoples, since we all carry forms of these weaknesses. Those listed below are only a sample list and, obviously, many more will be found during the course of our studies.

(a) Associative thinking.
(b) Reactive thought / thought linked to buffers.
(c) Thinking from a permanent centre-of-gravity called narrow self-interest.
(d) 'Mental-editing'.
(e) Thinking centre wrongly linked to instinctive centre.
(f) Thinking in extremes.
(g) 'Double-standards'.
(h) 'Fear-thinking'.
(i) Blame.
(j) Narrow judgemental thinking.
(k) Self-justification.
(l) Manipulation.
(m) Projection.

(a) Associative Thinking

This is where certain lines of thought (which are often very mechanical) are built up over time in an individual's mind, and form 'set pieces' to respond to different situations, ideas, concepts, people and so on. This type of thinking is *adopted* so that one *does not have to think for oneself* or *make fresh efforts of thought* when one comes upon new ideas, paradigms or impressions. We simply mentally reach into one of our many mental 'pigeon holes' and respond with a *prepared answer or solution;* without any *deep reflection or pondering on our part!*

This thinking originates in the mechanical or lowest part of the mental centre … the part we are meant to use for storing old ideas and not for responding to new ones!

(b) Reactive Thought / Thought linked to Buffers

This is where an individual has very strong views on a subject (usually wrong views) and <u>reacts emotionally and explosively when presented with an alternative view or paradigm.</u> This thinking also originates in the lowest part of the intellectual centre. It also demonstrates a wrong and maladjusted link to the negative part of the emotional centre. We all know someone who reacts in this way, when they do not get their own way or when a certain subject is mentioned. One may also recognize this characteristic in oneself at times; it is a negative trait which requires work and gradual elimination over time.

Buffers

In esoteric psychology, it is explained that a man very often carries within himself, very many opposite and contradictory views, opinions and emotional <u>stances</u> … but he or she never notices this phenomenon.

Why is this? This is because of the inner psycho-spiritual state of man today; we now possess certain 'psychological partitions' (called 'buffers') that keep contradictions in a person's psyche separated and intact. This, in effect, means that an individual may carry many opposing viewpoints or feelings internally, but never actually become aware of their existence.

It is said that a young child under the age of four has no buffers whatsoever and that buffers are only formed in the growing child through coming in contact with others who have buffers formed in themselves.

The more buffers we possess, the less we can see objectively in our life and in our society around us. Modern education produces many buffers in us!

<u>Self-Analysis</u>

> *'It is impossible for us to arrive at a judgment of ourselves through introspection – this judgment is sociologically conditioned!'*

> A.R. Orage. (11)

The buffer works by blocking us from seeing certain things in ourselves; certain contradictions, behaviour patterns etc. With buffers, we are only able to see one side of 'the coin' at a time; we cannot see both sides, as it were, simultaneously.

This presents us with a problem: we cannot see ourselves in the round; it is not possible to view ourselves completely or holistically.

We see many examples of buffers in people in society. We can see the man who goes to the Church or Temple, prays avidly, asks God to show him mercy and favour, then proceeds to go home and beat his wife until she is unconscious. If you were to reproach such a man for his actions, he will merely reply that it is his wife's fault for provoking him or for her misbehaviour.

One of the purposes of esoteric training is to remove these blockages or 'psychological partitions'.

(c) Narrow Self-Interest

When a person's thinking rests entirely with a centre of gravity of **self-interest,** then this individual is merely coming from one-centred thought. This represents a very immature stage of intelligence in the individual and one which shows that real inner-power is lacking.

An individual cannot become truly **balanced and integrated** with such a centre of gravity, psychologically and emotionally! This state in a person blocks further inner development in the objective and authentic sense.

It is necessary to go beyond this stage of narrow self-interest in one's life and begin to approach a new view of life and living. However, it is safe to assert that the majority of people in our society never go beyond this paradigm. If we remain in this stage, it prevents us from becoming truly balanced and doing many things on a holistic level:

- It prevents us from entering the position of another.
- It keeps us on a juvenile level spiritually.
- We do not expand internally and thus do not see 'the big picture'.
- We will never approach the paradigm of Higher Knowledge.
- Our level of mentation remains insular.
- We cannot develop Moral Force & Psychic Force.

(d) Mental Editing

This is a very interesting facet of modern thinking and one which is instantly recognisable to almost all people.

This means that, when you speak to a person about something arcane, deep or complex; they only respond to elements of your communication with which they are familiar and 'mentally edit' out the rest. This means in effect that <u>they do not actually hear core elements of your words</u>.

Often, should you meet them several days later, they will have absolutely no recollection of <u>the core substance</u> of your words but, instead, only remember some banal and warped version of what you actually said.

This is also a notable phenomenon where one individual points out the crass weaknesses or mistakes of another, perhaps in the best possible way; not as a criticism but as a friend. This is often met with in the same way, where core elements are 'mentally edited' out and the individual **will only remember what they want to remember** or feel insulted and slighted by their friend's remarks. Sincerity is missing in such an individual.

As it is said in the song:

'A man only hears what he wants to hear and disregards the rest'. (12)

(e) Thinking Centre Wrongly Linked to Instinctive Centre

Where the thinking centre becomes wrongly linked to instinctive centre, we see a situation where an individual 'only lives for comfort'; or, in modern terminology, they cannot leave their comfort zone.

This often means that an individual's centre of gravity in life becomes a 'comfort zone'; whereby an individual's life revolves around seeking pleasure on a continuous basis (the Pleasure Principle).

We find many people in our modern societies who are wrongly linked to the instinctive centre in this way. They do not like any kind of effort or obvious discomfort and will go to great lengths to keep their day-to-day activities firmly within 'a comfort zone'; a state which merely disconnects them from the clear vision and deep perceptions required to function as an intelligent Being.

Living in this mode disempowers people rather than empowering them!

(f) Thinking in Extremes

The logical mind has the very real tendency to think in extremes. A good example of this type of thinking is where one mentions a new concept to a logical individual and they respond with the same idea but in extremes.

This is a technique that the 'logical' individual will use to try to *invalidate* what you are indicating: often, advice you may offer as a solution to a problem!

This type of response is a type of sabotage ... it is designed essentially to undermine what you are saying; often where it does not suit the other person 'to go there' mentally or emotionally. It may be 'uncomfortable terrain' for them!

This type of exchange shows that the person you are dealing with is not at all interested in entering the sphere you have indicated. They are merely trying to discredit what you are saying by any means possible. You cannot take such an argument seriously; for it shows an unwillingness to be sincere and forthright on the part of the other person(s).

This type of mental behaviour can also be a 'habit of mind', where a person habitually thinks in this mode. It can also be used by the other person as 'a mind-game' or to try to aggravate! An example of this type of thinking can be shown by the following exchange:

You say: "A good exercise for an individual is to become independent from their family's influence, so that they have more freedom in their lives; and to stop their family from continually interfering in their personal affairs."

Response: (Logical / defective thinker – using an <u>extreme response</u>)
"I could never do that, since I would become cut-off from my family, loose all communication with them and end up miserable and alone!"

Note that there is also <u>a fear element attached</u> to this type of thinking which is very apparent! *(This is what the Sufis call 'fear thinking').*

(g) 'Double Standards'

This is yet another phenomenon easily identifiable in modern people and one which is most unpleasant to experience. I mention this phenomenon because of its importance and relevance to the subject in hand. It demonstrates a lack of inner-work on the part of the individual concerned.

'Double standards' as a 'Being' manifestation in modern people has many facets! One such facet is that of people who expect their friends / students / employees 'to be perfect' in every respect but who never apply these same exacting standards to themselves or perhaps to their own family!

There is the expectation of high standards and perfection from others, yet never meeting these same standards themselves; here there is a 'blind-spot'.

This phenomenon is also very visible in certain relationships; where a partner displays numerous exacting expectations, yet singularly fails to notice that they themselves possess none of these very qualities or abilities!

(h) 'Fear-Thinking'

'Fear thinking' is where one's thinking process is very often wrongly linked to the emotional centre – in fact, to the artificial negative graft on this centre; this artificial part of the emotional centre being particularly strong in such an individual. This is observable in individuals whose thinking process is often tinged with an exaggerated type of fear.

If one's reservoir of negative emotions in life expands beyond a certain limit, then these emotions begin to 'spill-over' into the intellectual centre, or the mind. This is a disease of the mental instrument, originating in the emotional centre. Its cause is that of gross impurities attached to the emotional centre of the individual.

It is explained in esoteric teachings that part of our initial inner-work is to purify our, too often, poisoned emotional centre. It forms one of the key pivotal platforms upon which much of our future work is based.

(I) Blame

Blame has become a prominent feature of modern thinking. We witness it in all aspects of life: from the old fashioned divorce system to governments who continually blame other countries for misbehaving and for failure. The strange thing is that the failure of others is often directly linked to our own failure.

For instance, we see many governments criticizing certain Third-World nations for lack of progress in development, when in reality this lack of progress <u>is often a direct result of massive interest on loans, which these same Third-World nations are repaying to developed countries; the countries which are doing all the complaining</u>!

Those possessed of a deep spiritual awareness are not so quick to blame others and can see how this aspect of modern psychology has almost become a reflex action in most modern peoples.

Blame has played a big part in the relationships between modern peoples; and blame is a strong feature of both logical and defective thought.

It is very necessary to go largely beyond blame in our thinking … the more awareness an individual has, the less old fashioned and naked blame will enter into the equation!

(j) Narrow Judgmental Thinking

This is where an individual is constantly measuring others according to imaginary artificial standards. Should the other person not meet these same artificial standards, then they are frowned upon and viewed as 'a lesser mortal'.

These artificial standards can include any of the following:

(a) Fashion / Dress.
(b) Wealth / Status / Class.
(c) Accent.

(d) Musical affiliations.

(e) Nationality.

(f) Job.

(g) Customs.

(h) Level of intelligence.

(i) Religion.

(j) Education.

(k) Background.

(l) Schools attended.

(k) 'Self-Justification'

When we do not wish to make the very necessary efforts to change ourselves in life, self-justification begins to manifest in our psychology.

When we are wrong, we self-justify. This is connected to the activity of buffers in us!

This type of behaviour in our mental-process is mechanical and not conscious! In other words, we are normally not aware of its action in ourselves.

It also shows itself when we want to cloak a wrong-doing and where we wish to 'leave the door open' to do the same again, sometime in the future.

This 'leaving the door ajar' to enable us to repeat the action at some future point in time, is critical here; since it is often the **pivotal** reason for self-justification in the first place.

Self-justification must be studied by us at close quarters; we must use esoteric knowledge and self-observation to see this phenomenon clearly in ourselves.

(L) Manipulation

Manipulation, the king of all mal-aligned thought patterns, seems to be endemic to certain types of people. At first, manipulation by others is quite often invisible, since 'it slips under our radar'. However, slowly, slowly, it begins to show itself and is quite often a very unpleasant experience.

We must also guard against this mind-set in ourselves; since, more often than not, we can not see it in our own psychological make-up!

Manipulation means <u>persuading others to do what you want by stealth and by a type of subtle psychological bribery or pressure</u>. People adept at this type of manipulation are not really interested in what you want – only what they want. The 'watchword' for manipulation is 'subtlety'.

(m) Projection

The psychology of projection is a very interesting one. When an individual becomes imbalanced psychologically or emotionally, one of the great 'tell-tale' signs is that they project their 'dark-side' onto others.

This means that an individual will project their own weaknesses, bad habits and psychological imbalances onto you and sometimes others. This also, of course, happens in many relationships; and, if it does manifest in a serious way with a couple, it may ultimately spell the end of that relationship.

Projection is a well-known facet of ordinary modern Psychology and has been recognized by same. It is a very strange phenomenon, because the person may appear very sane and otherwise completely normal; but, this is the 'big give-away' that all is not well and that this person is, in fact, emotionally imbalanced.

Notes

Section 5

Working on Personal Deficiencies

Working on personal deficiencies and strengthening our good qualities and abilities creates a wellspring of self-empowerment.

The list below merely contains suggestions for this purpose; many more may be found and listed during the course of one's life. However, the list below offers a sound working template for related future work and some may even adopt items from it.

- Karma-Yoga.
- Developing the four powers of Essence.
- Increasing our range of impressions – stretching ourselves.
- Self-observation & forgiveness.
- Communication / Empathy / Speaking Your Truth.
- Reciprocity.
- Working on inner-balance.
- 'The first-liberation'.
- Developing Moral & Psychic Force.
- Eradicating Lying.
- Metanoia – changing our perception.
- Developing the line of Knowledge.
- Group Work.
- Aims.

Karma-Yoga

The use of Karma-Yoga in one's life can be viewed as a very useful tool for inner-work. It is something which can be used all life long with a minimum of knowledge.

The common understanding of Karma Yoga is that of doing good deeds for one's neighbour or for those in trouble. However, this is really a tiny part of the overall remit of this very special and subtle spiritual modality. We can create strong character and good values by using this technique!

What is Karma-Yoga?

There are a number of elements to Karma Yoga, some of which are listed here for study:

- Helping others when opportunity arises.
- Meeting with unpleasant things equally with pleasant things.
- Working in the circumstances one finds oneself in!
- Pondering the reason you are here on Earth; the meaning of your life.
- Understanding that life is full of illusions.

> *'Throughout human history, as our species*
> *has faced the frightening, terrorizing fact*
> *that we do not know who we are, or where*
> *we are going in this ocean of chaos, it has*
> *been the authorities who attempted to comfort*
> *us by giving us order, rules, regulations,*
> *informing, forming in our minds their view*
> *of reality. To think for yourself you must*
> *question authority and learn how to put*
> *yourself in a state of vulnerable open-mindedness;*
> *chaotic, confused vulnerability – to inform yourself.'*

> **-Timothy Leary.** *(13)*

Karma-Yoga means right living. It teaches how to approach activity and the right relation towards people and the right action in the circumstances in which you find yourself in life. It is always interwoven with the concept of internal development & inner work.

One of the purposes of this concept is to fight against getting lost in *the stream of life's activity*; staying detached and with the awareness that all externals are really insignificant but cause us to *sleep spiritually*. We must cultivate detachment from external events. We must *be in the world; but be not of the world* – in other words, our core values and pivotal focus in life, must not be in the materialistic and mundane; our focus should be on the transcendent and the spiritual realms.

Developing the Four Powers of Essence

The four powers of Essence are qualities which each person needs to develop in themselves if they are to prevail in the work of inner-unfoldment and practical personal self-empowerment. These qualities can be increased in oneself by some of the exercises and items listed in this section. Just being intensely aware of these four powers of Essence can lay the very groundwork for later work and development of these basic qualities!

- Sincerity;
- Humility;
- Courage; and
- Tenacity.

Increasing Our Range Of Impressions

Increasing our range of impressions means going beyond our normal limits and stretching our life interests. We can only succeed if we step outside of the herd-mentality and go against our conditioning in life; this creates the unique backdrop for us to approach Truth.

This is not as simple as it sounds and all real self-empowerment involves the change of our way of thinking and ultimately, our way of life.

We have three types of food which our organism requires daily: the food that we eat; air; and impressions. Of these three, impressions are the most important food for us. Should all impressions cease to reach us, we would instantly die.

Impressions have the widest range of vibrations possible for us; in fact, we can absorb very fine impressions into our organism and store them there if we know how to do it.

Efforts & Receptivity

It is important to understand that, in this respect, there are two phases: efforts & receptivity. We must first of all be receptive to new ideas in life, new vistas and new paradigms for living; then, we must be willing to make the efforts required of us to achieve all that we learn and aim for.

Being receptive is a state of openness and readiness to explore; it is, to state the obvious, the opposite of being closed and rigid. So, we must explore in ourselves this facet of receptivity.

The Goddess Meditation

The Goddess Meditation is quite something to behold in practice, it involves 'invoking the Goddess', which is merely a force in Nature, to attract new things into one's life-sphere.

So we make contact with this force in Nature by sitting with a straight spine in a comfortable position, closing the eyes and focusing on an image of 'the Goddess' which appeals to your imagination or your mind. Then, simply visualize yourself as a 'human-magnet', attracting all kinds of positive energies to yourself – this can be spiritual, material, people, situations etc.

Self-Observation & Forgiveness

If we are to develop internally and in a real way, we must first understand certain things about our 'machine'. Many things block or get in the way of our inner-development; to this end we must work to remove these from our psychology. In the beginning, we use the technique of self-observation to isolate all of those elements in us which require changing and remedial work.

For instance, we must observe our emotional responses to others and to our immediate environment. With patience, we can observe our reactions and begin to change these over time! We begin to observe 'triggers' in ourselves and how some people and situations trigger us and our manifestations.

The realization that, when we react, we are no longer in control; others are; can be a big wake up call!

When we observe many defects in ourselves and realize that <u>we too carry many wrong and even sometimes offensive behaviour patterns</u>, we change our inner-attitudes towards life and towards others. We begin to be more fluid and more forgiving. We judge others less and respond in the positive to more and more situations.

> *'To be aware of a single shortcoming within*
> *oneself, is more useful than to be aware of*
> *a thousand in somebody else.'*

> **-Dali Lama.** *(14)*

Communication / Empathy / Speaking Your Truth

We find today many people who are in many respects quite capable, but who lack the capacity to communicate adequately. There are basically two aspects to communication: listening (empathy) and 'Speaking Your Truth' (the ability to communicate your deepest reality).

We should try to communicate positively on each and every occasion we encounter others, positive communication is one of the keys to a life of felicity and authenticity. This does not mean, of course, if we see something very wrong that we should not stand up and point it out!

Empathy

Empathy is the evolution in oneself of the quality of listening. This is a different kind of listening: a listening without judgment. It also involves the creation of a 'space' for the other person to speak or communicate. This will also imply such awareness as not 'speaking over' the other person or, not interrupting.

However, empathy is much more than this: *it is a quality of Being* which will demonstrate to the other person that you are trustworthy and competent, that you are a person of some real quality; aware and intelligent.

Speaking Your Truth

This is always an interesting subject to deal with because it means so many different things to different people.

At its core, it refers to *straight talking* and refusing to lie or fudge the issues. However, it can sometimes mean much more than this: it can mean that one must deal with very painful subjects; subjects which others may be opposed to even contemplate. At the heart of this is risk; you may be risking much to Speak Your Truth! It may require great courage beyond the norm to put your 'cards on the table' as it were; and so there may be a real element of courage involved!

Reciprocity

Another great principle in holistic and esoteric work is that of reciprocity or 'returning the favour'; treating others with kindness and generosity. It also holds meanings of exchange of ideas, communication, knowledge, insight, vision and creativity. It is also a concept connected with co-operation or co-operative movements.

In the cosmic sense, Reciprocity is connected to cosmic laws and how the Universe functions; the reciprocal action of everything existing in our Universe. All particles or bodies in nature exchange energy continually; a good example of this is our Solar System, where all the planetary bodies exchange energy all the time. This also happens between the Earth and the Moon; and between the Sun and the planets. So, we can see that reciprocity is also a cosmic principle and one which, if observed by man, profits everyone without exception.

Humanity was designed by Great Nature to be a reciprocal species, and, without this all-embracing principle, we are cut-off from many positive forces.

Working on Inner-Balance

One cannot work for high spiritual advancement without first working for real and practical inner-balance, both psychologically and emotionally. That is why it is said, one cannot 'build a castle upon sand'.

Creating inner-balance in oneself is of vital importance and requires some amount of genuine pondering; we will look at this in more detail in the section called 'The Spiritual Autopsy'.

Some of the elements to be considered when looking at inner-balance:

- Control over the emotional-centre.
- Considering others.
- Developing self-knowledge.
- Moral Force.
- Psychic Force.
- Freeing oneself from the opinions of others.
- Neutralizing the False-ego.
- Recognizing false-interests in oneself.
- Cultivating authentic understanding as opposed to 'head-knowledge'.
- Changing our attitudes.
- Speaking one's Truth.

> *'However much you study, you cannot know without action. A donkey laden with books is neither an intellectual nor a wise man. Empty of essence, what learning has he, whether upon him is firewood or books?'*

> *Saadi of Shiraz. (15)*

'The First-Liberation'

The first-liberation in life, according to esoteric teaching, is that of freeing oneself from the opinions of others.

When we are free from other people's opinions of us, we are free of other people. This is, of course, a principle which can really only be observed in action.

A good example of this is where a couple are living together as partners and one partner continually discusses the couple's problems and decisions with their family or parents. Now, the other partner is, in practice, having a relationship with a host of people; not just the person they have married or settled with.

This is why it is important for a person to develop a level of maturity in themselves which precludes such problems arising.

Working on Moral Force & Psychic Force

In general, these forces or abilities are missing in modern man; both of which were intended by Great Nature to aid in our development and natural spiritual evolution.

Moral Force:

The Moral Force in man represents the distillation of qualities and principles in life by which a person lives; through their own efforts.

For the modern mind-set, this is somewhat difficult to understand; since man believes he already possesses all the qualities he needs and lives by the highest principles. However, this is simply not so!

Esotericism tells us that Moral Force cannot be engendered in man by the use of ordinary data and influences available to him in ordinary society. It requires Knowledge and influences of a higher order.

Therefore, a good working definition of Moral Force in man is the distillation of qualities and principles from life; through his own efforts, using Higher Knowledge and influences as a main directing force or catalyst.

Psychic-Force:

This is the ability in man to see beyond the ordinary influences around him in life to perceive those higher influences, which are often found in a fragmented form and mixed with the influences of ordinary life. It also involves the ability to *see into other people* and to discern accurately their qualities, their character, and if any *'cloaking'* is present!

If education is too strong in a man, he looses his natural ability to perceive these higher influences in life!

Lying

The subject of lying is of major importance to inner-development. It is approached from the perspective of developing sincerity in oneself by a new kind of thinking and a new kind of training.

The thinking and training is, of course, esoteric. We can see, when we are open and without self-deception, that society is in many ways artificial and out of step with people's needs. Our overwhelming need is the development of our Essence, our innermost Being; society does not, under ordinary outer conditions, provide us with the impressions, materials or Knowledge we will require to achieve this.

Mundane society creates personality in us but cannot educate, refine and develop our inner-core: Essence. When our personality is rendered passive or weakened; when we are not so besotted with externals and when we begin to develop a new vision of life and living, personality of itself begins to weaken. At this point, we witness a portal of opportunity beginning to emerge, an opportunity to develop Essence and real qualities in ourselves. Lying and personality are directly linked. Because man lives almost completely in personality he is very much removed from that which is real and transcendent – his life is vague and rather meaningless; full of missed opportunities and profound, authentic life experiences.

Because lying is so prevalent in our cultures today, we can never approach Truth or hope to get a glimpse of the sacred in our midst, save by following a different Path – we have to bypass the mundane in order to connect to that which is real and meaningful. This is the task of every truly intelligent person … bearing in mind that academia and intellectuals do not equate to *intelligence!*

> *'The miraculous is very difficult to define; for me this word had quite a definite meaning – I had come to the conclusion a long time ago, that there was no escaping from the labyrinth of contradictions in which we live, except by an entirely new road unlike anything known hitherto or used by us. I was unable to say where this new or forgotten road began, I already knew then as an undoubted fact, that beyond the thin film of false reality, there existed another reality from which*

for some reason, something separated us. The miraculous was the penetration into this unknown reality.'

P.D. Ouspensky. *(16)*

Metanoia – Changing Our Perception

In order to change our Being, we must first change our way of thinking; this will ultimately change our actual perception of things. This is called *metanoia* in the Bible and wrongly translated as 'repentance'.

It is ultimately our perception which can change the direction that our life is taking; or not. We can only strive towards something special if we can first of all perceive it. Without this altered and deepened perception, we remain static and our real position, in terms of consciousness and Being, does not move.

The ancient people of our world were aware of the possibility of change in man; the potentiality of heightened consciousness and developed being:

> *'... Egyptian High Priest, Manetho, who had access to unlimited ancient texts from the ancient library at Alexandria, and who wrote for the Pharaoh, the history of ancient Egypt in 30 volumes, makes reference to the divine beings that ruled during pre-pharaonic Egypt.'*

Utopia – Buz. **[Internet Quote]** *(17)*

So, the key in the beginning is to change our perception, to alter the neural-pathways in the brain to allow for a new paradigm to enter and take root. This new paradigm is that of *esotericism*. The Knowledge and understanding which esotericism provides brings a new, third force into the equation: a new catalyst which alters the structuring and perception of the brain.

This third force of esotericism can change how we receive impressions, how we deal with life situations and also how we treat others. This is, one might say, the first manifestation of this new force in ones life. Later, with effort and momentum, we can radically change our perceptions and how we take life; our aims, aspirations etc. It is a 'learning curve' like no other.

<u>A Brief Note on Impressions:</u>

The subject of impressions is of vital importance to us here. The real value of impressions is missing in ordinary society. <u>Impressions are energy</u> - energy which comes to us within a range of very dense vibrations to that of incredibly fine vibrations. This fine range of energies is of particular interest to us; since it is with fine energies that we build our internal world.

Under ordinary circumstances, we take in only very coarse energy from the Universe. However, we have the capacity to absorb incredibly refined energy into our organism and fix it there. It is, of course, fixed in our energy body and not in our physical body. This process <u>completes</u> an individual; because higher consciousness requires a refined vehicle to anchor in our organism!

<u>Example of Impressions:</u>

Other human beings are impressions for us: we see them, we communicate with them and we react to them.

Firstly, there is the acceptance or rejection of impressions; and then comes the 'digestion of impressions', which is quite similar to the digestion of food. This means that you take in certain parts of these impressions and excrete or get rid of other parts.

We have briefly covered this aspect of impressions in our section on 'Mental Editing'.

In modern-day Psychology, they have a term called 'Cognitive Dissonance' which is very similar to that which we are speaking of here.

Normally, the organism takes in impressions which are at a level of relative coarseness; but these can be transformed upward to form more refined energy if a *new force* enters the equation at the point where they enter. This new force is our *line of Knowledge.* To develop our line of Knowledge means in this instance that we need to acquire new Knowledge.

Developing our Line of Knowledge

Although we cannot develop internally without a catalyst and a very special type of terrestrial Knowledge, people still believe that ordinary practices will somehow suffice in this sphere.

To this end, we must develop our line of Knowledge; that is, we must actively study the ancient Knowledge of our planet, Earth; the Knowledge which gives insight into the practical development of Man's inner world. This must be done through effort and with intelligence and not merely hoped for or, anxiously awaited to arrive in our laps. We are architects of this type of sourcing and use of ancient wisdom; we must understand the difference between active and passive study.

Passive Study:

This is to study with only a fraction of our real capacity as a human being. This type of study happens when people read novels, newspapers and magazines etc. Passive study is mechanical, intellectual, and uses only the lower divisions of centres. Passive study <u>does not nourish Essence or help it to grow and mature</u>.

Active Study:

This is a totally higher order of magnitude in relation to study. Here, one has to use more of one's Being to absorb and understand the 'big-picture'; to try to connect seemingly unconnected parts into a cohesive whole.

- It brings the emotions into study, connecting the emotional and the mental centres.
- It means <u>understanding</u>, rather than 'memory recording'.
- It means deep contemplation or pondering.
- It allows new impressions to enter the equation.
- New paradigms are not instantly rejected.

This new force thus created, if we allow in new impressions in the form of new ideas, will enable us to approach life differently; to organize these very same impressions differently in ourselves.

You will learn to take in a relaxed and gentle way that which most people would take in a very negative way; and you will learn to take things in a serious way that which most people take lightly.

In the beginning, we understand things only superficially – we do not understand them deeply. This is, of course, a process and one which takes time to develop in oneself – it does not happen overnight.

A Higher Order of Knowledge:

Essentially, we are talking about a Higher Order of Knowledge – one which is both on a different scale and which has a more refined *substance* than that of ordinary terrestrial knowledge.

It is also the case that people find it difficult to approach Higher Knowledge, to begin with. *One must learn from those who know!* Understanding increases gradually until one can *see a complete and cohesive vision of what this ancient wisdom really means and what it is telling us.* There are no short-cuts in the beginning.

Positive Ideas:

It is through positive ideas alone that a person can grow internally. Negative ideas, which abound in society, can never increase a person's interior stature by a single micron.

We see negative ideas all around us in society, in the media and in the News. Negative ideas only serve to drain our force; whereas positive ideas provide us with new force for life and for exploration.

The most powerful and authentic positive ideas and principles come down to us from ancient times, via esoteric teachings. These teachings, which are basically uncorrupted in their structure and nature, are not to be found on the surface of our civilization but exist only at its core, and have to be traced. It requires work and patience to understand their significance and power – 'we are like little children in a game meant for adults!'

Group Work

It is imperative to understand the importance of group work for our personal self-empowerment and indeed for the empowerment of others similar to ourselves. Group work magnifies our active work in this sphere, allowing others to mirror the work which we need to address in ourselves and vice versa.

One of the primary facets of this addressed by group work, is our family and cultural conditioning. In this, we are faced with many new demands and models of thought. We meet with entirely new mind-sets, different than our own, and face situations where we must move into Essence in order to grow and mature internally. To this end, group work is designed to create a space wherein the person can grow at their own pace whilst learning from others and contributing, themselves, to the crucible of Knowledge & understanding. Caveat: ensure that any esoteric group you join is *authentic* in the full sense of this word and not just another cult!

Big Dilemma No. 1   Cynicism

To begin with and, depending on the individual, cynicism is the big 'bogey man'. Cynicism is actually the flip side of the intellectual coin – it represents the negative side of our critical faculty. The opposite of being superbly understanding and our having a critical mind, is that of being cynical. Cynicism destroys so many positive good things for us, it deprives us of a correct evaluation of things and, also, puts a negative slant on almost everything we touch.

Avoid being cynical!

When we are cynical we can never approach the subject of our own hypnosis and conditioning. This cynicism is a prominent psychic feature of many modern people. In order to evaluate the paradigm of social conditioning in detail, we must, firstly, be able to think and evaluate without being cynical.

Big Dilemma No. 2   Ignorance

We lack objective data from which to base judgments on our psychic status and the conditions of society. This is a universal practical problem for the average man or woman in the street. There is, in the ordinary scheme of things, no real data available with which to compare society's input into our psychology and world-view.

> *'It is impossible for us to arrive at a judgment of ourselves through the mind or introspection - this judgment is sociologically conditioned!'*

> A.R. Orage. (18)

We are educated to believe that we have all perspectives, all points of view and all forms of thinking possible for Man. We are taught that science will ultimately solve all our problems and that there is really no need to search or look elsewhere for answers. Even in modern psychology, philosophy and sociology, we are guided away from asking certain *core questions,* looking at life from radical perspectives.

We are encouraged to learn how the minds of the past perceived and dealt with these *core questions* but we are never really encouraged or taught how *to think for ourselves.* Everything is taught from a top-down hierarchical structure; with many questions and answers prepared in advance, with little room to construct our own vision of life and learning.

Education:

In the past century, we have had many great secular thinkers who have stepped forward and given us a new understanding of what education should be like. Foremost among these were John Dewey, Palo Freire and Thomas Khun. We also had Jean Piaget, a foremost thinker of his time, who brought us very close to esoteric thinking on education.

Although it does not fall within the remit of this module to go too deeply into these brilliant *avant garde* thinkers and reformers, we will look briefly at some of their words and ideas.

Let us take John Dewey to begin with – and what later became known as 'progressive education'.

> *'The term progressive education arose from a period between 1890 & 1920 when many Americans took a more careful look at the political and social effects of vast concentrations of corporate power and private wealth. Dewey's passion for education is deeply linked to the idea of a democratic society. For Dewey, the deepest meaning of democracy is the dignity and worth of each human being, and its moral demand that each person should be treated as an end unto himself.*

> *'According to Dewey, the importance of personal growth for the individual in society has been largely ignored, when the freedom of growth and free development are restricted. Based on the*

criticism of traditional education, Dewey developed the theory of progressive education and focused on personal experience and experiment. <u>Progressive education is mainly based on the student-directed model that teachers are no longer the authority of knowledge but as instructors who help students to explore their own uniqueness; their purpose and goals for learning.</u>'

Dewey also stated:

'The progressive educators should respect and allow individual differences and treat a learner as an end, and encourage his capacity to develop a mind of his own.' (19)

Jean Piaget (1896 – 1980)

'J. Piaget established the foundational idea of psychological constructivism in the 1960's and it set up a revolution, in distinguishing itself from the epistemological tradition of Western civilization. Instead of accepting that knowledge is objective, constructivism claims that knowledge is temporary, developmental, non-objective, internally constructed, and socially and culturally mediated. It is generally accepted that there is a great deal of resistance against this view of knowledge, and of scientific knowledge in particular. For more than 2,500 years, the Western philosophical tradition has perpetuated the notion of human knowledge as a more or less 'true' representation of a real world. This view has dominated for the realists, for whom the essence of science lies in the collecting of 'objective' data which, they believe, speaks for itself and automatically provides a true explanation.

'Thus, knowledge is ready to be discovered and scientific knowledge is the method and result of those discoveries. Nevertheless, Piaget stood on a different side, arguing that knowledge has to be seen as a collection of schemes of action and models of thinking that allow us to live and move in the world as we experience it. Science is the product of a thinking

mind's conceptualization, and a tool of adaptation. From this perspective, knowledge does not represent or depict an independent reality but a collection of theories that happen to fit the world as it is experienced.' (20)

What is revolutionary and pivotal in all of this, is that Piaget is saying that our much vaunted science is not at all objective. A theory is 'hatched', only to be replaced a decade or so later by another theory, and so on! What is strange is that nobody seems to have noticed this simple and self-evident phenomenon before.

Piaget's biggest contribution to modern times was perhaps his contribution to the substance and structure of how education should be. He demonstrated that children require a different approach in their education than that of adults. A child's cognitive development requires a radically different approach, using sensitivity, understanding and a willingness to listen to the individual child's needs. Children should not be educated *en masse*; in a rigid, mechanized and regimented fashion. This method, developed by Piaget, is very close to that which we now term 'holistic education'.

Education is 'a top-down' phenomena, where everything is handed down by government at its base or inception and is designed and implemented from the standpoint of vested interests. In other words, education today is not in any way objective or without interference; it is, rather, a product of the State designed to produce <u>artificial consensus and maintain the status quo</u>!

Our education is, in reality, highly choreographed and controlled. People spend their whole life navigating through our various social strata and never even suspect this. It is the perfect paradox. It is perfectly true; but people are unable to hold this truth in their consciousness for very long, because of the very nature of living in this *highly hypnotic socioscape.*

This was demonstrated by Paolo Freire, perhaps the most radical secular thinker in the past hundred years.

'I suggest Freire's Pedagogy of the oppressed provides us with a critical perspective to investigate the problems of contemporary science education, by examining the tensions between the

teachers and students in this model of education which he called "banking education". He argued that banking education has reinforced the "vertical pattern characteristic" of education and "anesthetizes and inhibits creative power" among learners.

'Freire criticized the narrative character of education and he referred to the teacher student relationship as a narrator –receptacle model; teachers play the role of narrators, and their job is to fill the receptacles with narrated content, while students become containers that mechanically memorize the narrative.

'Furthermore, according to Freire, banking education has a character of depositing: the teacher is the depositor and the students are depositories. In this context, "filling" becomes the goal of education; as Freire wrote, "The more completely she (the teacher) fills the receptacles, the better a teacher she is. The more meekly the receptacles permit themselves to be filled, the better students they are". The education is no longer based on a process of communicating between students and teachers, but it is the teachers who decide upon, prepare and make deposits to the students who are expected to "patiently receive, memorize, and repeat".

'The concept of banking education is very similar to transmission education and both of them refer to a hierarchy of knowledge transfer, in which educators remain on the upper levels and the learners stay on the very bottom of the hierarchy. This model is also famously associated with the expert-to-naives model, indicating that knowledge is transferred from those who have to others who have not.

'These education models have been criticized for placing the educators and the students into two ends of a process of knowledge distribution, and the students' potentials and *capabilities are largely ignored. Similarly, Freire pointed out that the role of the teacher in banking education is problematic, and that "the teacher confuses that authority of knowledge with his or her own professional authority, which he or she sets in opposition to the freedom of the students".*

'In Pedagogy of the Oppressed, Freire strongly criticized banking education, arguing that "education is suffering from narration sickness"; students become the collectors of what they are told, but lack "creativity, transformation, and knowledge in this (at best) misguided system". The more students obey the imperative to store the deposits, the fewer creative and critical capabilities they develop; the more they accept the passive roles they take, the less they develop the critical consciousness to challenge the system and to transform the world. As a result, they become "adaptable, manageable beings". Freire also considered the educator-student relationship as oppressors– oppressed, and he argued that the aim of banking education is not to transform the world for the better, but "lies in changing the consciousness of the oppressed". By controlling consciousness, the oppressors are able to "regulate" the ways that students enter the world; in other words, by controlling the minds of students, the oppressors can preserve a profitable situation they have benefited from.' (21) [Chingfang Chang]

'Education is a system of imposed ignorance.' Noam Chomsky (22)

Big Dilemma No. 3   Fear of Alienation

Fear prevents us from confronting many things in life. It prevents us from facing reality; what's out there or what is hidden from us. This also includes social inconsistencies and façades. Our biggest fear, in relation to very close scrutiny of ourselves and our sociosphere, is that of being somehow 'left out of the game'. We fear, if we enter too deeply into the cause and effect of things, that somehow we will have to deal with the resulting distasteful and disquieting findings. We may never have peace of mind again.

We also fear that our friends may desert us and we might find ourselves alone. We may become a social outcast, shunned by those around us for having exposed uncomfortable truths and unpalatable discoveries.

Big Dilemma No. 4   Comfort

Deep down, we know that the social paradigm or structure in which we live is somewhat crazy and exudes deep incoherence, blind alleys and false pursuits – but at least it is familiar and we can derive some amount of comfort from it.

Our comfort would most certainly be affected, were we to decide to *stand against the flow* and scrutinize things in a fresh light. Could we bear the contradictions?

We would be forced to realign all our old views of ourselves and, of the society we live in; this might turn up many unpleasant facts and emotions previously buried or suppressed.

And finally, *we have invested so much emotionally in society* – we have placed our hopes and future vision of ourselves firmly entrenched in society, playing a definite role, adopting social norms and affirming standard views.

Is it possible to question all of this, is it possible to *go against the flow* and question the status quo? If we want to grow spiritually, the answer has to be yes! Without changing our way of thinking, our perception never changes and without changing our perception, we will never mutate internally!

COURAGE

'Courage is the greatest life quality, everything else is secondary. You cannot be trusting if you are not courageous. You cannot be truthful if you are not courageous. You cannot enquire into reality if you are not courageous; hence courage comes first and all else follows!

'It is only out of fearlessness that love can arise. It is only out of fearlessness that one can go into the enquiry of the ultimate! It is a long voyage, and it is a voyage into the unknown. Cowards won't be able to leave this shore. And awareness means a great longing for the other shore which is not visible from this side.'

Osho. *(23)*

Aims

Finally, we come to the subject of aims. This subject is of the utmost importance since, without aims, one does not actually move forward but just move in circles.

Formulating one's aim can be the single most important task a person can do in life, for it creates a centre of gravity focus to work towards, each and every day.

One should always have, in general, two aims: a small aim and a larger, long-term aim, if you like. One must begin with a small aim; something which is attainable for you; something within reason, and then work towards our much bigger aim, which is in the future. The smaller aim, in reality, may be a number of small aims which are connected and, in effect, which work towards the larger one. This is always a good formula for success.

Aims can be mundane or spiritual, or indeed a mixture of both. Below, I have given an example of a spiritual aim which one might formulate:

1. Big Aim:

• Develop complete mastery of myself spiritually over time.

2. Smaller Aims:

• Develop understanding of esoteric principles.
• Meet people similar to myself who share these higher aspirations.
• Work incrementally everyday, and build a foundation for future work.
• Draw up a plan for the year and work at implementing it.
• Learn new skills in the fields I am interested in!
• Involve myself with authentic groups, so that I may learn valuable lessons.

It is important to understand how <u>vital</u> aims are; because, where we do not formulate aims, we often find ourselves going around in circles and not moving forward.

Tips For Dealing With Our Deficiencies

- Accept that we all have deficiencies and that they can be overcome with awareness and work.
- Work at sincerity and seeing weaknesses in oneself without self-deception.
- On occasions, allow close friends to be frank with you.
- Group work.
- Set staggered and realistic aims.
- Learn to relax.
- Work at conquering violence in oneself.
- Learn to forgive.
- Make a study of fear both in others and in yourself!
- Devote some time to working on negativity, moods and self-pity.
- Tapas Acupressure Technique for: emotional trauma, addictions, limiting beliefs, physical trauma, eating disorders.
- Suggested Reading:
  Maurice Nicoll, *Psychological Commentaries*
  P.D. Ouspensky: *In Search of The Miraculous*

Notes

Section 6

Taking Back Your Power

The subject of giving away one's power is an important theme in today's world. We find ourselves inadvertently giving away our power in too many situations and in too many ways.

There are many situations in life where we give away our power; I have listed some of them here.

Examples:

- Gurus.
- Co-dependency.
- Never complaining.
- Being 'a doormat' in a relationship or a friendship.
- The 'victim' syndrome.
- Being constantly negative in life.
- Being subservient to our boss to an unreasonable degree.
- Allowing friends or relatives to dominate us.

There are, by contrast, many situations in life where we can take back our power from others or from situations; here are some of them listed below.

Examples:

- Leaving a violent partner.
- Standing up to a bully or if your child is bullied at school.
- Standing up to your boss if he or she is taking advantage of you.
- Not accepting sexual harassment!

- Making <u>your own decisions and acting upon them</u>!
- Breaking away from parental karma and control.
- Checking the contents and ingredients in the foods we consume.
- Not leaving a tip should we decide the service is rubbish!
- Voicing our true feelings in a situation which we feel is wrong!

Some writers, like that of Liz Adamson, 'hit the nail squarely on the head' with her enlightened take on the subject of personal power:

> 'First I need to differentiate between external and inner personal power. Virtually all the examples we have of power would involve the former. We see it in politicians, dictators and those with money, status or position that can be wielded over other people. We may associate this sort of power with corruption and sleaze. Those with external power will often render other people powerless. Those who seek external power will often do so because they are not in touch with their own inner power.

> 'Personal power does not seek to dominate or negatively affect others; indeed, it will work to empower those around us. Our personal power will work to generate the energy needed to create what we need and want in our lives. If we do not have this we may feel stuck or stagnant. Nothing happens and we may feel tired and apathetic a great deal of the time. The less energy we have to send out, the less will be able to come back to us in the form of opportunities, miracles and gifts.'

> Liz Adamson. (24)

There are very many forms of giving away our personal power; some of these include giving our power away to a lover, a bully or a religious figure in society.

With the lover, we give our power away because we want something in return: love! With the bully, we give our power away because of fear to do the right thing. With the religious figure, we give our personal power to them because we believe that somehow they are spiritually superior to us and that they may intercede for us with the higher-powers.

Personal power is also connected with boundaries and how we construct and maintain our boundaries. If our boundaries are weak, then we will be the plaything of others and of many situations. Constructing and maintaining our personal boundaries with others is very important. It is our natural right to have strong and well defined boundaries with others; otherwise people may intrude into our personal space, like a thief, and demonstrate their keen lack of respect and even hostility towards us.

A very good example of personal inner power was that of Mahatma Gandhi. Gandhi did not derive his power from outside; from any position or from any title; his power emanated from within. His concept of satyagraha, meaning devotion to love and truth, through non-violence, being the core of his principles for life!

Gandhi held real convictions and real inner power because he had spent years in India, solitary, studying himself and the nature of Cosmic Truth. He was a man of self-knowledge devoted to Truth & justice. Gandhi had both Moral Force and Psychic Force at his disposal when he negotiated with the British Empire for an independent India.

The Man with Inner-Power:

A man imbued with inner-power has a great thirst for Knowledge and for self-Knowledge; he understands the need for universal peace, harmony and justice. His highest inner quest is to set out on a voyage of discovery and to innovate. He has a great respect for all women and shows this at every opportunity. The natural environment is very important for him both in terms of conservation and enjoyment; absorbing all the good energy from nature being a very important facet of his existence.

He is capable of speaking his truth and will not shy away from this, when the situation demands it. He will not always choose the path of least resistance and will often follow a course which may seem to others, difficult and thankless.

The man of inner-power has conquered violence in himself; he will not be provoked easily and considers violence only in self-defence situations.

This man will carry genuine compassion for others and real empathy too. He is never too busy to stop and help a stranger in distress, because he knows that, in reality, beyond social convention he and the stranger are one!

He also has a great power of adaptive thinking or *thinking outside of the box*. He is good in a crisis and will not hesitate when others freeze from fear or self doubt. He is courageous. He is not interested in *having power over* others or controlling people in a self-interested fashion. He does not need to be controlling in order to feel good about himself; his motivation comes from a set of internally generated principles and not from culture-bound attitudes and prejudices.

The Woman with Inner-Power:

A woman with inner power is expansive, understanding and holistic in outlook. She knows her own worth, strong points and limits.

She respects life, the environment and also the opposite sex. She expects this basic respect in return. She is not 'phased' by other women, even if they are more beautiful and attractive than she is. She has no dispute with womanhood.

Her power is not in how she looks; her power comes from within, she is grounded in the Earth and has no quarrel with her body! Her intuition is strong and she uses it to navigate life's many 'mine-fields'.

The woman of personal power works on her negative states; knowing they are a source of disempowerment rather than something to be enjoyed.

She has an empathy which shows her how all life is connected and how all life is somehow interdependent, even though logic does not allow for this. She avoids dominating others or being dominated herself; freedom is her basic intrinsic value.

She is communicative and nurtures real friendships, rather than being manipulative. She recognizes the dangers of 'the Dark Goddess'.

She is creative in more than one mode and uses creative thinking to move forward in life! She is not afraid to speak out when a situation is unjust and she refuses to comply with social fears and restrictions of culture.

A woman with personal power will only partake of the essentially healthy elements from her society / family / culture; the rest she leaves behind.

She will not be bullied into submission, but may sometimes retreat in order to re-group. She believes in the universal rights of all peoples, from all countries and backgrounds; and especially those of all women, wherever they may be.

As she gets older, she becomes the *wise woman* and is sought after for advice and blessings from many in her community.

This woman comes from substance and not just style; in other words, more and more from Essence and not just Personality.

A New Kind of Dynamic Power

Here we are really talking about a new type of power: not *power over* but inner personal power, which does not come from power in society or from without. This power is not about domination, it is not about control and it is not about manipulation.

It is about awareness! It is about vision and profound intelligence slowly manifesting in a person until perception is completely changed beyond recognition. It is about opening ourselves to the mysteries and *incredible awe* we are filled with, when looking out on a clear starlit night and just being present. It is about *standing alone* if necessary, with no one to back you or take up your cause. *It is about courage!*

Tips For Taking Back Your Power

- Avoid conflict but at the same time do not give in to the domination of others. Learn about your rights and civil-liberties; for example, it can be of great use to study The United Nations Charter on Human Rights and The European Convention on Human Rights!
- Never think that you are powerless to change something or a situation; search for a solution which does not involve giving your power away.
- We can sometimes give our power away to addictions, false interests, our career, hobbies, partner etc.
- Never hide your confidence, abilities or qualities from others, just to keep them from feeling insecure or 'threatened'. Let your confidence and self-esteem illuminate the way for others to do the same!
- Giving your power away to members of your family is very common. Break the pattern and liberate a vast amount of creative energy.

- Help others to reclaim their personal power, to be creative, independent & freethinking!
- If someone is manipulating you, resolve to draw up a plan or strategy to neutralize such a situation. Seek advice from close friends you can trust.
- Do not feel helpless with such people as mechanics, builders, lawyers, estate agents etc. The moment you view them as 'professionals who know more than you', you are giving away your power. Always get everything in writing and always get a second quote or a second view on the problem/ situation.
- Do not be intimidated by doctors or medical practitioners; they are also human and make mistakes. Doctors often intimidate their patients with negative suggestions, such as "oh well, if you refuse to take the medicine you might die". Check out alternative treatments for your condition, such as Chinese medicine, Reiki, Homeopathy, etc.
- Never give your power away to politicians; politicians are just people, no matter how lofty their aspirations or promises seem to be. They often conceal hidden agendas, personal interest and third parties in the background.
- Literature:
-
  - 'What Doctors Don't Tell You' (Lynn McTaggart)
  - 'A Woman's Herbal' (Kitty Campion)
  - 'Courage – The Joy of Living Dangerously' (Osho)
  - 'Coleman's Laws: The twelve medical truths you must know to survive ...' (Vernon Coleman)
  - Books on psychic protection.

Example of a Woman Who Took Her Power Back

'Emmy Noether was a German mathematician who made groundbreaking contributions to abstract algebra and theoretical physics. Albert Einstein described her as "the most important woman in the history of mathematics."

Her work on differential invariants in the calculus of variations, Noether's theorem, has been called "one of the most important mathematical theorems ever proved in guiding the development of modern physics." Under Nazi Germany she was forbidden from teaching. She refused to accept this, and continued to teach in secret.

Taken form website: 'I fucking Love Science.'

[Women you should have heard of]

Notes

Section 7

Cleansing the Emotional Centre

Probably *the most important element in the beginning* of esoteric work is that of cleansing the emotional centre.

Because of man's abnormal existence in today's artificial society, many natural functions in his psychology have gone astray. Today man can best be described as a negative entity, with negative moods, anger, fear and jealousy dominating his psyche.

It is of such importance, that it requires specific mention here. Many of us in life just accept negativity, anger, violence and moods as part of life and part of what we must put up with. Indeed, in relationships this is often true. However, what is not understood is that the negative part of the emotional centre is not a natural construct. In other words, there is no natural function in the emotional centre which is inherently negative. It does not exist. What actually happens is that *an artificial graft is formed* in this energy centre, by what is called mimicry or the influence of others being negative around us. This begins in childhood!

It is one of the most important malfunctions of modern man's psyche – a situation which has created a type of hell for the modern individual.

One of the central tasks for the novice to esoteric work is the cleansing and purification of the emotional centre. This requires careful study and diligent awareness. A specific understanding of what this means for the individual and its ramifications (which, by the way, are many and deep) is required by those who seek to elevate their Knowledge and their Being. The deepening of Essence cannot be achieved without this work. <u>Our emotions carry the key to our inner evolution!</u> Our emotions are directly **anchored** in our Essence. This is what Gurdjieff says on the subject:

> *'It must be noted that the organism usually produces in the course of one day, all the substances necessary for the following day. And it very often happens that all these substances are spent or consumed upon some unnecessary and, as a rule, unpleasant emotion. Bad moods, worry, the expectation of something unpleasant, doubt, fear, a feeling of injury.' (26)*

Manifestations and Secondary Manifestations of an Imbalanced Emotional Centre:

- Emotional outbursts / the Dark God or Dark Goddess.
- Projecting : 'You are a very negative person'
  (Often a very negative person will project their own condition).
- Undermining behaviour.
- Sabotage & self-sabotage.
- Selective amnesia.
- Lying / avoiding emotionally painful truths!
- Cloaking: hiding emotional dysfunctions from others.
- Jealousy.
- Moodiness.
- Anger / violence.
- Spitefulness & grudges.
- Certain types of manipulation.
- Controlling behaviour (being a 'control freak').
- Certain addictions: i.e. to food; overeating.
- Noticeable negative reactions in a person to small things.
- 'Fear thinking': thinking from a fear-based mind-set.
- Neurosis.
- Certain types of irrational behaviour.
- Hatred.
- Impatience.
- Certain types of irrational insecurity.
- Self-pity.

- Certain types of cynicism.
- Blame used as a destructive psychological weapon.
- Negativity can act like a contagion and spread to other people quickly.
- Revenge.
- Harassment.
- Humiliation of another person.
- Depravity.
- Exploitation of others.

Negative States and the Resulting Chain-Reactions:
Moods, Negativity, Anger, Resentment etc.

- Blame surfaces.
- Big Picture of Life Disappears.
- Lying Begins.
- A feeling of being wronged.
- Understanding Ceases or Diminishes.
- Moving into Mechanical or Lower Parts of Centres.
- Hatred Builds.
- Revenge Comes into the Equation.
- Internal Considering Begins.
- Person Stops being Reasonable.
- False-Personality or Superficial-Self Emerges.
- Compromise often Disappears.
- Double Standards are Often Apparent.
- 'I am Right and You are Wrong' syndrome.
- Other People become the Enemy.
- Collective Energy-Field changes to Negative Energy.

When we enter negative states, a strange chain-reaction happens to us and we begin to act and speak in a way which we would not normally do. It happens at a speed which our mind cannot pin-down and we find that we have to later repair the damage caused to our relationships with others!

'In the sphere of the emotions it is very useful to try to struggle with the habit of giving immediate expression of all one's unpleasant emotions. Many people find it very difficult to refrain from expressing their feelings about bad weather. It is still more difficult to express unpleasant emotions when they feel that something or someone is violating what they may conceive to be order or justice.'

G.I. Gurdjieff. *(27)*

Negative States and Negative Emotions

As we enter the subject of negative emotions, we enter new terrain and 'uncharted waters' for many. It will require a whole new look at how we normally understand negative emotions and various other states.

We Do Not Have Positive Emotions!

In our ordinary lives, we do not possess what might be termed positive emotions. These are not possible for us, in our present state of Being. There exists the real possibility, however, for us to control some if not all of our negative emotions.

Positive Emotions Means Being Connected With Our Higher Centres!

One of the most prominent features of negative emotions is the energy loss factor. We loose a huge amount of energy when we get angry, sad, frustrated, jealous, loose our temper, pity ourselves etc. In fact, this loss of vital psychic energy can leave us deficient for the rest of the day. A single burst of extreme bad temper may kill-off most of our quality emotional energy for that particular day.

As the human machine stands, we have barely enough energy to fuel our psychic life as it is (the chakras); but when a massive drain ensues, we are immediately in trouble.

The whole concept of negative emotions and the struggle against their expression plays a huge role in authentic esoteric learning. The higher learning teaches us that it is imperative for us to struggle with negative states and our expression of negative feelings. This inner struggle will not come to fruition immediately but over time and with increased understanding and diligence.

Further, we need to come to the understanding that all negative emotions are really useless; that is, they cannot ever have any use or benefit for us.

'We have the right not to be negative.' **Gurdjieff.** *(28)*

What is generally not understood is that negative emotions are not at all obligatory for us; we can be free of these states and change our inner and outer response to external stimuli met with in life.

The struggle against our negative states can not begin directly, but must be done indirectly on many fronts. It begins by studying the core ideas which explain this psychic maladjustment in our lives. There are a number of things which one must work on, in order to defeat these states and manifestations.

In modern Psychology, it is stated that is harmful to the individual to resist negative emotions and hold them inside. Since modern Psychology can only use the medium of logic, and lacks the insight of esoteric wisdom, it would seem that, as regards defeating negativity in a person, it is at a complete loss. It gives advice for the temporary relief from such feelings but not for their long-term and complete eradication.

Indirect Work on Negative Emotions:

- Change our attitudes to these emotions and their instant expression.
- Reverse our primitive psychology of narrow self-interest.
- Develop empathy with others and the ability to place oneself in another's position.
- Karma Yoga.
- Seeing one's own weaknesses without 'the blinkers'.
- Understanding that life is your teacher and each day is a test.
- Seeing oneself in another and them in you!
- Learn as much as possible about these states from the esoteric perspective; this leads to real understanding and the development of a new force in oneself.

Only when one has begun to work on many lines of work at once is it really possible to halt the manifestation of negative emotions, without any dire consequences for oneself. In other words, normally, when we shut down a negative habit in our machine, it is very quickly replaced by another negative habit of a different nature. In this case, no new negative habit will be formed to replace the one defeated; because it is carried out <u>consciously</u> and not by blunt force or repression.

One of the more noticeable side-effects of being in a strong negative state is that we cease to be reasonable; we become intolerant, we lie and we are <u>not aware of this</u>!

We even say and do things which are contrary to our normal way of life and our normal way of being. Later, we often regret these things which we have said and done, being lost as to how it all came about.

These things happen because, firstly, we enter a lower state of awareness; and secondly, we are not in control!

Perhaps the most important element of negative emotions in us is the fact that we make excuses for them! We self-justify when we are negative; we may say something like, 'You made me angry'; or 'It is because you did not wash the car that I threw that tantrum'. It is necessary to be aware that negativity does not come from another person; it comes from you and it is a major weakness. It is usual to have both blame and self-justification at work when we make excuses for our own negativity.

> *'According to the Work teachings, we are not born with negative emotion; they are sown in us through imitation of our elders during infancy, and by the gradual encroachment of the everyday world, with its false values and objectives. By the time adulthood is reached, the emotional centre is a mass of negative emotions ....'*
>
> *Harry Benjamin. (29)*

The next thing to understand is that when we become negative or moody and do not resist becoming so, we put ourselves instantly under more and more laws. We are less free and we suffer as a result; the problem being that we become addicted to this mechanical and abnormal condition; and even though we are suffering, we continue with this absurd behaviour in ourselves.

So it is that we need to work especially hard on this problem of negative emotions and mood swings. In many instances, it will ruin friendships and relationships over time. We need to recognize it for what it really is and take action to remedy the situation in our manifestations.

One of the many mechanisms which contribute to this problem is that of building up complaints, criticisms and judgments of others, regularly and over time. These bad feelings towards another person eventually form a critical mass within us and, one day, this person comes along and this build up of bad feelings erupts and we direct a tirade of negativity towards this other.

This build up of negative feelings and judgment forms a dark and dense energy within us and its natural dynamic is to be released. In other words, this energy is by its nature uncomfortable to hold internally and we release it when the opportunity arises. We do not see how this build-up of negative force is down to ourselves and not to the other person. It takes time, pondering, and also practice to see this in real-time situations. However, its complete and unequivocal comprehension is pivotal to our inner work and to changing the status quo.

> *'Anger is an acid that can do more harm to the vessel in which it is stored, than anything on which it is poured.'*

> -Mark Twain.

Another form of negative state is that of worrying and one which is very destructive for our life and normal functioning. One of the facets of worrying is the fear that we have no control over our life or of some facet thereof. When we build qualities and abilities in ourselves through conscious efforts, these worries begin to recede into the background:

> *'Everything changes when you start to emit your own frequency, rather than absorbing the frequencies around you,*

when you start imprinting your intent on the universe rather than receiving an imprint from existence.'

-*Barbara Marginiak. [Internet quote] (31)*

Meditation

<u>Buddha meditation for forgiveness and compassion</u>

Meditate on people who have created anger, fear, jealousy, hatred in you and visualize yourself in their presence and forgive them for wrongs and injustices you have suffered at their hands in the past. Do this even though it is very difficult and thorny. Then, reverse the meditation and ask those people whom you may have hurt in the past for forgiveness.

(This is a daily meditation – if you have forgiveness issues or remorse).

Tips For Dealing With Negative Emotions

- Notice how negative states deplete you of energy and vitality.
- Notice how others trigger negative emotions within us.
- Notice that we loose control.
- Notice that, in some respects, this puts others in control of us.
- Observe how we often feel embarrassed afterwards.
- We even become angry, <u>even more negative</u>, because of this.
- Observe these 'triggers' internally and how their mechanism works. <u>Often, it is only our self-image which is offended!!</u>
- Observe internally that, with some of the lesser irritations, we can shut them down with a little awareness and determination.
- Make a resolve not to be 'triggered' or 'controlled' by others or by situations which are adverse.
- 'Externals are harmless in themselves' – Ouspensky
- After mastering minor irritations with others, or difficult external situations, move to more difficult irritations incrementally until you come to those situations which are the most difficult for you.
- Lastly, choose a critical irritation and 'make this your god' to defeat!
- Be aware that the struggle against negative emotions must be done in tandem with all of the other items indicated earlier in

this section; and must be carried out over time, with patience and awareness. Tackling negative states head-on can have numerous contrary results.

Make a conscious decision not to be annoyed by the remarks of others. 99% of all such remarks are designed to undermine and not as constructive criticism or informed / aware advice!!

Notes

Section 8

The Spiritual Autopsy

When we become aware of the very real nature of the mechanical influences which surround us in life, it soon dawns upon us that we need to separate ourselves from many of those negative influences which harm us or store up harm for us for the future; like a 'ticking-time-bomb'.

There is also the factor of where we are going in life, what meaning we derive from life and what holds most significance. This often brings us to the subject of our aims in life; which are often blurred and unclear. It will sometimes become apparent to us that we need to clarify our true aims and direction in life.

This is where the 'Spiritual Autopsy' comes in!

It is suggested that, at the age of 20 or 21, one should engage in a fresh evaluation of one's life; taking an honest look at where one is at and where one is going. The Spiritual Autopsy means examining carefully, and with real sincerity, all such factors in one's life; and devising methods to counter negative influences and enhance positive elements in our lives. This is not as difficult as it might seem; many people on diverse spiritual paths, and even in ordinary life, undertake this task on various different levels and with varying degrees of success!

It is often necessary to examine dispassionately and with ruthless candour our own motives and the motives of friends and family around us, their influences and the influences of our sociosphere or culture.

Regardless of age, one should consider the 'Spiritual Autopsy' exercise as a means of evaluating one's own inner psychic landscape and how one fundamentally relates to life.

We also need to look at what is called 'The Three Levels of Karma' and how these affect our lives. The study and understanding of the Three Levels of Karma will help us gain insight into our life and to view the different subtle influences which surround us that so often exert a disproportionate influence on our perceptions, our decisions and world view.

The Three Levels of Karma

1. THE KARMA OF ONE'S PARENTS' INFLUENCES.
2. THE KARMA OF ONE'S FRIENDS' INFLUENCES.
3. THE KARMA OF ONE'S CULTURE'S INFLUENCES.

DEFINITION OF KARMA

'Every real effect must always and everywhere strive to re-enter its own cause!'

With the Three Levels of Karma comes the Knowledge of how our own innate psychology and emotional cognition is formed in us. We begin to glimpse how certain influences and patterns have been implanted into our Being over time.

> 'Be aware, that the science which provides the bridge between the inner and outer life of an individual, is rare and is transmitted only to those who have been prepared beforehand.
>
> 'It always happens, that there will be many who will prefer to accept imitation in place of reality; the superficial in place of true wisdom.'
>
> *Hadrat Muinudin Chisti. (32)*
> *(Founder of the Chisti Order in India)*

1. THE KARMIC INFLUENCE OF ONE'S PARENTS

This type of karma pertains to such items as: expectations, manipulation, pressure at school originating from parents, fear of one or both of one's parents, wrong ideas about life passing from parent to child etc., etc.

This type of karma can and does have a strong adverse effect on young people. Many young people develop psychological problems or even personality disorders as a direct result of negative parental pressure. This is <u>the hidden side of parental karma</u>. Unfortunately, this naive negative parental pressure routinely comes from defective thinking and is very often <u>fear-based</u>. A chain of this type of thinking and behaviour is often passed down through generation after generation in certain families!

Other forms of negative parental karma include parents deserting their children at a young age, teaching their children wrong values for life; and physical, emotional, psychological and/or sexual abuse.

There are also sometimes more direct parental karmic effects in the form of hereditary traits and tendencies transferred to an individual. These can vary from alcoholic tendencies, violence and depression to physical traits and disposition.

Positive Karma

Then, of course, there is the positive karma from parents, where parents have brought up their children with wisdom, love, dignity and authentic understanding. In some respects also, the parents will have separated their children from negative influences through wisdom, proactive and positive communication, and by example!

And lastly, the transference of this wisdom and understanding to their young at every stage of their development is of vital importance.

Caveat

There is, of course, one major caveat here: what most parents in today's Society consider wisdom, positive communication and example, are simply not so. Also, it must be mentioned here that no developmental teaching can be done through manipulation, lies or coercion – this will always prove counterproductive.

2. THE KARMIC INFLUENCE OF ONE'S FRIENDS

The karmic influence of friends, especially for young people, should not be underestimated. Obviously, much influence exerted by friends on young people is positive; but some is definitely of a negative nature. This negative influence can sometimes continue right into adulthood.

On some occasions, the pattern of a person's life may be changed for the worse by the adverse influence of peers. Some obvious examples are the use of illegal drugs, alcohol, smoking, pornography and violence.

Some of this can be directly connected to gang culture or just blokish / girlish behaviour. Gang culture is a particular phenomenon for parents to look out for; since most parents of young people who belong to street gangs are unaware of their belonging to such gangs. The karmic effects of gang culture are of a particularly pernicious nature and represent an even stronger threat to a young person than most other forms of delinquency.

There are also many more, subtler negative influences transferred to young people by their peers. These may include negative modes of thought, addictive negative emotions and less obvious behavioural items such as laziness, apathy and neglect of personal health and wellbeing.

In some cases, mental health problems can be traced all the way back to a single incident occurring while a young person was in the company of peers – e.g., while engaged in substance abuse or the like.

Another facet of the karmic influence of friends is that of our mind-set, i.e. the mind-set we adopt for life and living. This includes our attitudes, emotional stances, prejudices etc.

3. THE KARMIC INFLUENCE OF ONE'S CULTURE

The karmic effects on our life and mind-set from our culture are quite substantial, significant and all-pervasive.

Every culture which has existed on Earth and indeed in every epoch has had its own mind-set, or paradigm. According to esotericism, our current Epoch represents a 'low watermark' in terms of culture, vision, banality, shallowness and hypocrisy. This situation arises primarily because we now function mostly in the false-ego and not from *the original blueprint* intended for us by Great Nature; that is to say, we do not function from a mature and educated Essence.

In our modern culture, the way people think and view life are a direct product of their environment; their culture. <u>People no longer think for themselves</u>. People confine their thinking within well-defined social and cultural parameters. Man has been robbed of this ability by a vacuous culture, one which perpetuates false values, greed, false-interests, destruction, exploitation and violence – all cloaked in fine words!

Exercise

Over the following blank pages, we will carry out a short exercise, which may serve as a catalyst for a future 'Spiritual Autopsy'.

On each page, list the items of positive and negative karmic effects you may think are relevant to you, taking time to ponder the issues deeply. This exercise is designed to help you think in a different mode about your life. It can also prove surprising what will come up with an analysis of this kind; items which we may never have considered pivotal or of substance in our lives may show themselves in this small scale exercise.

Firstly, at the top of the page, list all of the positive karmic influences and, then, at the bottom of the page, list all of the negative karmic influences. These items noted down can, if you so choose, remain private. It is your choice if you decide to share them with your friends or not.

> *'Understanding and knowledge are completely different sensations in the realm of Truth, than they are in the realm of society. Anything which is understood in an ordinary manner about the Path is not understanding within the Path, but exterior assumption about the Path, is common among unconscious imitators!'*
>
> *Buhaudin Naquashband. Counsels of Bahaudin Naquashband.(33)*

With judicious choices and an awakening of awareness, karmic forces in our lives can be changed and modified. But in order to do this, it is first of all necessary to bring into awareness all the karmic modalities at work in our personal life-sphere!

We can go on living as before or we can make radical, life changing adjustments. We can filter out many negative elements and factor in, positive life enhancing elements to our lives! This knowledge comes to us from esotericism and not from any contemporary jaded academic modality; which in reality, will always pale by comparison and can never give us anything real!

1. The Karmic Influence of Our Parents

Positive Elements:

Negative Elements:

2. The Karmic Influences of Our Friends

Positive Elements:

Negative Elements:

3. The Karmic Influence of Our Culture

<u>Positive Elements</u>:

<u>Negative Elements</u>:

Tips For Carrying Out A Spiritual Autopsy

- Find a quiet place where you will not be disturbed.
- Use the previous exercise to initiate the process.
- Do not predetermine the outcome.
- Suspend fear, self-criticism and narrow judgmental thought.
- Remember: this exercise is private and no one else will see it.
- Be ruthlessly sincere and honest about everything.
- Ponder your own motivations.
- Ponder the motivations of others.
- Keep in mind that the outcome may be very positive indeed for your future decisions, life-plan, aims etc.
- Use a diary or other pad which you will keep safe and away from the eyes of others in your circle.
- Be creative.
- Use your intuition.
- It may take more than one sitting to complete.

Notes

Section 9

Fulfilment / Meaning in Life

In order to talk about meaning here, it is first necessary to study closely just what 'meaning' is. We all, of course, believe we know what meaning is; but the reality is that this is far from correct.

This subject of meaning in life is of immense value to us in relation to life and what we wish to achieve in our life. In order to be empowered, we must find fulfilment and meaning in life. The trick is, one can find a temporary meaning in many things and be temporarily fulfilled; but, can one find a truly permanent meaning and thus, long-lasting fulfilment? This is the question!

What people do not notice in their lives is that meaning changes for us all throughout our lives. When we are in our teens, perhaps music has the most meaning for us; in our twenties, perhaps our work has the most meaning for us; and later, in our thirties, we may only find meaning in [**relationships or**] our own personal development. <u>Generally, people only have interests and not real meaning in their lives</u>. Below we find seven principles which held meaning for the extraordinary Bruce Lee -

1. *As you think – so shall you become.*
2. *It's not only increase but daily decrease – hack away at the unessential.*
3. *Learn about yourself in interaction. To know yourself is to know oneself in action with another person.*
4. *Take no thought of who is right or who is wrong or who is better than. Be not for or against.*

5. *Avoid a dependency on validation from others. I am not in the world to live up to your expectations – and your not in the world to live up to mine.*
6. *Be proactive. To hell with circumstances – create circumstances.*
7. *Be yourself. Always be yourself. Express yourself – have faith in yourself.*

-Bruce Lee. [Internet quote] *(34)*

From the esoteric perspective, there are two types of meaning in life: that of meaning in relation to Essence; and meaning in relation to Personality. In other words, if we live continually in Personality, our interests are going to correspond to this level; we will have 'worldly interests'. Unfortunately, these mundane interests mutate over time, without our even noticing it. This creates an illusion of fulfilment.

On the other hand, these interests and limited impressions cannot nourish Essence. Essence is left in limbo, with no *food for growth!* This is the ultimate conundrum of modern life! In our ordinary life, meaning *is not a stable datum but mutates over time!*

In order to derive a permanent meaning and fulfilment from life, something else is needed; we must find a meaning which not only does not change but which grows in substance and significance for us. This is the quality of meaning required to nourish Essence; we cannot live by society's *norms* and expect to grow internally – this is not possible. Meaning found in society cannot help our inner-world to expand; this is like putting a soft-drink in our fuel tank and expecting our motorcar to drive as normal. It is the wrong fuel!

Generally speaking, self-empowerment comes from Essence – from a well-formed, well-developed Essence in man. Nothing can replicate this. It is a prerequisite. In ordinary life, meaning is transient!

> *'The Universe is always speaking to us … sending us little messages, causing coincidences and serendipities, reminding us to stop, to look around, to believe in something else, something more.'*
>
> -Nancy Thayer. *[Internet quote](35)*

So, real meaning can only manifest through the path of genuine essence development and unfoldment – nothing else is going to cut-it! All else is an illusion on a grand scale. Essence is that which is real in us – the divine spark which is talked about in all religions, in all ancient lore on the subject: our liberation is bound-up with this 'seed', this same 'mustard-seed' that is mentioned by Jesus in his parables to the people. This 'mustard-seed' can become a tree – a latent something becomes a manifest something, a great mystery alluded to by Jesus Christ.

Next, the question arises: how does one approach this new paradigm of high Knowledge, fine impressions and the growth of Essence in life itself? Is there some kind of starting point or key?

A change of perception is required and, in order to change our perceptions, we must learn to think in a new way.

The Four Levels of Thinking

- Defective thinking.
- Logical thinking.
- Psychological thinking.
- Esoteric thinking.

• Defective Thinking

Defective thinking is a function of the formative part (mechanical part) of the intellectual centre in man. Defective thinking is always based on wrong thinking and inadequate assumptions. An example of defective thinking is where a person bases all of his or her decisions on whether <u>they like</u> this or that person, this or that colour, this or that voice. What could be described as decision making <u>on a whim</u>.

• Logical Thinking

Logical thinking is a function of the whole of the intellectual centre in man. This kind of thinking gives better results for a person – but it is far from perfect. Its modus operandi is usually to compare this or that, black or white, this lady's looks with that lady's looks, search for 'facts' where one should adopt a holistic approach. The logical person does not realize that, very often, last year's facts become this year's fiction, in ordinary life.

- **Psychological Thinking**

Psychological thinking is the result of three or more centres in a man, functioning in unison and, not only this but, the higher parts of these centres. One cannot approach Higher Learning without being able to access psychological thinking in oneself; and it follows from this that the purely logical individual can never follow or understand the person who has the superior ability to think in the psychological mode! It is from this mode of thinking that *real meaning in life can be accessed!* It breaks the mould of conventional linear thinking and frees up potential perception and emotional cognition. This is the level of true understanding and real inspiration.

> *'When you are inspired by some great purpose, some extraordinary project, all your thoughts break their bounds: your mind transcends limitations, your consciousness expands in every direction and you find yourself in a new, great and wonderful world – and you discover yourself to be a greater person by far than you ever dreamed yourself to be.'*
>
> *Patanjali. (36)*

- **Esoteric Thinking**

Esoteric thinking represents what is often termed in esoteric psychology as 'all centres balanced state'; and, not only this, but all seven centres working together on a certain level. With further development, all centres *function as one centre.*

Esoteric thinking is not 'thinking' as we commonly understand it: it is thinking on a higher level (a new state of consciousness). It is also, at times, referred to as 'The Witnessing Consciousness' or 'Self-Remembering'. It is the third state of consciousness possible for man and one which is his natural state or birthright.

For the purposes of this course, we will focus on that of our ability to engage psychological thinking. <u>Psychological thinking brings us new impressions</u>.

With the advent of psychological thinking in the individual, comes a new phase of empowerment and life meaning. We begin to question the status quo. Only through continuous questioning and, of course, <u>asking the right questions</u> can we move forward.

Modern Education

Esotericism tells us that, in modern peoples, our education and development is lopsided; we do no longer feel what we know with our whole Being!

Our knowledge is always that of external things, and it is always a very partial knowledge. We have, for instance, no knowledge of our own inner-world, nor of our potential for inner development. *Our education is merely one-dimensional, when it should be three-dimensional;* we cannot extrapolate from our modern education any 'substance' or material which would serve to nourish our inner-world.

<u>Modern education only provides us with an intellectual veneer, and one which will never serve our real needs in life</u>! So it is that we have to look beyond our 'education' to another way to achieve this end. <u>True education nourishes our spirit and not just our mind</u>!

Esotericism explains that man has much greater capacities and abilities than we commonly understand. However, we cannot access these higher abilities in ourselves because of our malformed development. This is why it is said that education; its modern structure and modality, is so malevolent for our unfoldment and development as terrestrial beings.

The structure of our modern education strengthens Personality and weakens Essence. Personality is rendered active and Essence is rendered passive in man. Now, in order for a human being to develop, the reverse must begin to happen: Personality must, at a certain stage of its development, be rendered passive and Essence must be allowed to grow. Only with a real growth of Essence can a man or woman grow internally or spiritually!

And so, all that is false in man … all that is acquired, all that is not his own, if you like, is exalted by modern education. Man's chakras are not opened in him uniformly, and so, the data for engendering *objective reason* in him, as designed by Great Nature, does not take root. Thus, man's manifestations in general all remain mechanical and out of kilter with his *true nature*.

Now, it is well know in quantum mechanics that you cannot solve a problem with the same mind-set which produced it. One has to go beyond the old mind-set and 'think outside the box'. This is where the Second Education comes in and this is where *psychological thinking* comes in!

It is only when we see modern education for what it really is, that its meaning changes for us. That is, our relationship to it changes; we do not want to engage with something which is pernicious and out of step with our true needs as human beings.

Of course, there are always exceptions to such a rule and sometimes people may have to 'ford the stream' to get to the other side. By way of example, we see young people 'cramming' vast amounts of data into memory, ninety per cent of which will never be used or useful to those students in their later life. We see students 'swatting' for exams under stress and under duress from parents. When this happens, very often the young person's mental health is affected adversely and we see a steady decline in such a person's overall health, physical and spiritual.

Most of what young people learn today in schools is forgotten very soon afterwards. We see an increase in depression and loss of self-esteem among a large segment of school populations, with suicides on the increase among teenagers, where many problems are related to modern schooling; such as bullying.

> *'However much you study,*
> *you cannot know without action.*
> *A donkey laden with books is neither*
> *a wise man or an intellectual.*
> *Empty of essence, what learning has he -*
> *Whether upon him is firewood or books?'*

> *Saadi of Shiraz.*

'The Educated Fool'

Today we have an entirely new phenomenon at large: 'the educated fool'. The individual who has much 'education' but little ability or Being-qualities. People who 'know much' but who can do little. Unfortunately, this type is very suggestible and cannot discern the superficial nature of our education system nor the fact that there are different levels or qualities of knowledge. To them, all knowledge is the same; it just deals with different aspects of life.

It is through the current vacuous 'education system' that this situation has come into being. 'Educated fools' are *a product of the system* and they are unable to free themselves from the *psychological blinkers* imposed by the system. It is for this reason that we see very little change in society and witness only tiny structural changes and *no changes of substance* or to the *underlying fabric* of society.

> *'Education is a system of imposed ignorance!' Noam Chomsky. (38)*

The Second Education

The ancients speak of a 'second education' possible for man. This quality of education does not rely on logic; does not rely on thought control, as with our modern-day education system. It does not mould the neural pathways in a person in a narrow way but opens neural pathways of an expansive mode.

Many models of current modern-day thinking cannot be part of a second education: 'profit at any cost'; 'the end justifies the means'; 'science is always the best measuring instrument'; 'them and us'; 'a top down hierarchy of teaching'; 'do not question the system'; 'education will get you everything you want from life'; and many more. These models of thought in today's society actually prevent us from learning in a holistic and natural way. We are continually 'steered' down a path which precludes deep questioning; and also perpetuates the moving away from fundamental cognitive improvement. In today's system of education, the answers are provided to us before we even have a chance to formulate our own questions. Thus we are given simultaneously, both the questions and the answers – an absurd situation. Essentially, we are, in real terms, discouraged through both structure and content, not to think deeply and not to think for ourselves!

Today's scientists say that we use only one-tenth of our brain's capacity; we do not use the vast majority of our brain power. The ancient wisdom tells us that 'we live in the basement of ourselves'; and that, to access our full potential, we must be prepared to step outside conventional modes of learning and undo the programming caused by orthodox education and social convention.

We need to connect with our inner-self; this is the real secret to finding real meaning and fulfilment in life. A connecting with our inner-self means a disconnection with our false-ego. Modern values, education and our social norms cannot connect us to this inner-self or Essence.

> *'The fact is that the only way to fill the space inside us is to connect with our inner-self and feel the, peace, harmony, wisdom, joy and insight that this part of us brings. Our inner-self is indirectly connected to the absolute. We can only have our needs met if we are connected to the Source of all. If we are not in touch with our inner-self, we are allowing our superficial-self or false-ego to guide and rule our lives.'*

> Liz Adamson. (39)

So, we can see that real meaning in life comes from an unexpected source: from the depth of our own inner Being. The only question remaining is how we can access this meaning. True fulfilment cannot come to us from the outer world; something is always missing. So long as we are removed from our inner-self, all of our 'education' and social conditioning, which for the most part remains in Personality, will constitute only an intellectual veneer!

We need to develop using 'three dimensional learning' or what is called **The Higher Learning.** We need to engage <u>all</u> of our inner psycho-spiritual tools called chakras, in a balanced and uniformed way. Only this approach gives us the possibility of, firstly, becoming balanced individuals in life; and then secondly, the possibility in later life of working on a deep spiritual level.

Our approach to learning today is both startlingly naïve and incredibly childish – we are still *living in the dark-ages* when it comes to knowledge!

> *'Knowledge is generally confused with information. Because people are looking for information or experience, they do not*

131

*find Knowledge. You cannot avoid giving Knowledge to one
fitted to receive it. You cannot give Knowledge to the unfit,
this is impossible. You can, if you have it and, if the person is
capable, fit a person to receive Knowledge.'*

Sayed Najmuddin. (40)

This second education can provide a new paradigm for learning, eventually changing our cognitive abilities. By introducing ideas and principles of a higher order, this new praxis will provide the framework for many to change their lives on a deep-structured level. Our emotional field and apperception is elevated to a new level. There is also the opportunity to change our Being.

Below is a further example of a new idea which can serve to demonstrate its great scope, value and veracity.

*'When I realized that the ancient wisdom had been passed
down from generation to generation for thousands of years
and came to our days almost without alterations, I regretted
that I started too late to give such knowledge the immense
significance that I now understand it has.'*

G.I Gurdjieff. [Internet quote](41)

Gurdjieff searched for almost twenty years before making contact with a *root-circle of masters,* he had intuited that these people of a higher order than ordinary humanity must exist – this forms the first principle of esoteric lore. This first principle is that everything existing in the Universe has a core; the atom has a nucleus, every galaxy has a black-hole at its centre, the Earth itself has a core made of metal, each person has a spirit inside, every country has a core called government, every school has a core called teachers, every community has a core in the form of the principles and values they abide by and so on.

Humanity also has a core and it takes the form of evolved human beings; those who have developed beyond the level of the collective!

The Three Sacred Impulses For Man

Description of the three sacred-impulses – engendered by Great Nature:

- Self-Preservation.
- Reproduction.
- Self-Perfection.

Self-Preservation

This sacred impulse is no longer strongly defined in modern day peoples. Why? The reasons for this are manifold, with perhaps not a single defining reason! Contributing factors are: cities, police, modern social habits and the decline of man's natural instincts. Self-preservation manifests in many and varied different forms – castles, lake-dwellings, tree-house, cliff-caves, all kinds of weapons and the like.

The emergence of martial arts is also a major facet of self-preservation. We have developed very sophisticated methods of self-defence, using much diverse weaponry, including firearms. Today this impulse is not as well defined in modern man as, say, in ancient times; we now rely on someone else to protect us: the police, the army, the 'Guardian Angels' on the tubes, our friends and even our neighbours! Generally we do not take much time to develop such skills or instincts; partly because of the speed and tempo of modern living; and partly due to our attitudes towards such issues – e.g., we can now let the police handle our day-to-day safety.

Needless to say, this is something of 'a false economy', another one of our many social illusions.

Reproduction

This sacred impulse is present in almost all terrestrial Beings, starting young and manifesting strongly upon reaching puberty. Sex is probably the most developed and pronounced impulse in the modern world. Sex or what might be termed the reproductive instinct will generally be present, while the force of self-preservation may be absent.

The problem with sex in today's world is that it has virtually turned into a kind of commodity. Sex is now used from advertising ladies' fashion accessories to the biggest blockbuster movies. Sex when used in this way becomes 'infra-sexuality' – that is, a force which takes on board many banal, negative and manipulative aspects. It adds to social conditioning with the abuse of the true meaning and significance of sexual energy; sex is no longer considered sacred.

<u>Self-Perfection</u>

This last of the three sacred impulses for man on our list, happens to be the most important but, also the one which is most atrophied in men and women of today's world.

The sacred impulse for self-perfection is of singular importance to all of us; without this impulse, there would be no hope for the Earth! Beneath the surface of modern man's consciousness is buried *the impulse to self-perfect;* but, it must be stressed, *it is buried very deep.*

On the surface, we project our petty superficial and sensory consciousness outward, in the form of needs and wants. This projection of energy outward holds the key to the impulse of our own perfection. Our energy constantly projects outward and downward and, as the ancient Alchemists have pointed out in the distant past, <u>we become a mere conduit for cosmic forces to pass through</u>. This 'energy-pump' must be reversed! We cannot do this without first awakening *the sacred impulse to self-perfect!*

This brings us full circle in our journey to understand meaning and true fulfilment in life; it cannot be achieved through material things alone!

Through the assimilation of esoteric wisdom and new Knowledge, we create new meanings for ourselves in life. Out of the ashes comes the Phoenix.

Meaning Disappears

We do not see, normally, that at certain points in our life we enter a crisis. This happens because what formerly held meaning for us, now loses all meaning for us. It is as if, in our normal life, what we had formerly held in great store and what we were formerly emotionally anchored in vanishes suddenly and we are left bereft of meaning. This does not mean that all crises in life are connected with meaning; but it is very often true of our mid-life period, where former meaning disappears and we are left in a type of vacuum. This is called <u>a mid-life crisis</u>.

We have all heard of the mid-life crisis and some of us have experienced it. It is, of course, a very unpleasant experience. It is often the fist time in life, for many, where meaning in life comes to the fore and is examined with some anguish.

In reality, we should be examining meaning in our life, throughout our life. Were we to do this, it is very possible that we would have crossed this painful Rubicon in our youth and thus have circumvented the problem.

The *core problem* is, however, that without an *outside agent* we cannot view this whole subject of meaning 'from higher ground'. In other words, we <u>cannot place anything in perspective</u>; we cannot measure what really troubles us, because it is unquantifiable! This is what is painful; we do not even know where to start, our emotions are in turmoil, our thoughts have no *traction,* we are lost 'in a sea of meaningless contradictions'.

We cannot think our way out of the situation as we formerly did when we were younger. What has happened?

What has happened is that all of those things which we have formerly put so much emotional investment into, now cease to hold any importance at all for us. Our problem is basically an emotional one! What is this new *outside agent* mentioned above?

As you may already have guessed, it is the line of Knowledge we can use and develop in life, if we are wise enough to engage it. This engagement develops <u>understanding and changes our 'emotional field'</u>. <u>We Change</u>!

Tips For the Process of Introducing New Meanings Into One's Life

- Regularly go beyond your normal limits.
- Incremental risk taking.
- Make contact with people who possess greater knowledge and wisdom than you.
- Allow old meanings to die, such as false-interests; in order to make room for new meanings to enter your life.
- Adopt a new spiritual practice.
- Travel.
- Look at what has *real meaning* for you in your life.
- By contrast, look at what *has no meaning* for you in life!
- Counselling from those on the Path.

Notes

Section 10

Vasanas

Here, we come to the subject of Vasanas – or *patterns in our being* and in our life in general. We are highly conditioned entities, with filters and thought control introduced into our life through a number of artificial conditions, of which modern education is but one.

Our patterns of thinking and feeling are directly influenced by our culture and people around us. Our artificial social constructs serve to implant filters in our minds and direct our emotions towards subjects which are of little objective value to us.

Because of this situation, much of our potential as human beings is dissipated and rendered passive. We have become <u>passive participants</u> in a world pregnant with ideas and meaning, but hidden from our view <u>by socially imposed 'blinkers'</u>. Cinema is one good example.

Should we follow the narrow dictates of our modern society, then we will find ourselves in a spiritual wasteland, with no real beacon of hope for the future. Everything is artificial and contrived; with manufactured and well tailored appearances which have been perfected over centuries; we are duped into accepting a veneer of shallow facades and half-truths.

Because we are part of this artificial society, we carry components of this continuum within us. The first task is to see that this is actually happening around us and to refuse the deception. This does not happen all at once but takes time and patience to achieve. <u>We must see this clearly before change can happen</u>!

Many of our self-limiting beliefs were implanted in us over time and through the framework and influences of our immediate society. We often develop hidden negative views of ourselves because of this.

> *'One of the reasons why many of us do not embrace our optimal lives even when they are presented to us, is because there is a deep seated belief that we are not good enough or deserving enough of good things coming to us.'*

> *Liz Adamson. (42)*

Generally we presume many things about ourselves which simply are not true. These assumptions, more than anything else, block us in our inner and outer development. We assume many qualities and abilities in ourselves which we do not possess; or which we have, in reality, yet to develop. Only with sincerity and humility can we redress the balance, re-arranging our inner world, so that our outer world can manifest in harmony and simplicity. We must ascertain accurately and with ruthless honesty, our real strengths and weaknesses; then begin to work on these. We must work at increasing our strengths and neutralizing our weaknesses, over time and with increasing vigour.

Engrams

Engrams are strong subconscious imprints engendered in the psychology of an individual either by repeated and reinforced ideas or a traumatic event.

Engrams are 'the small print' of our psychic lives. They represent all of the psychic factors and hidden mind-set in man which rarely show up on the 'social radar'. Their 'social signature' can be recognized by strange and unpleasant manifestations in a person, which signal, like a periscope cutting through the surface of water, that there is a submarine beneath.

Manifestations such as prejudice, malice and racism signal the presence of these engrams: e.g. engrams such as feelings of superiority, which carry a whole raft of negative manifestations such as sexism, bullying, violence, rape and murder. On a lesser plane of behaviour, they manifest as crass undermining behaviour, manipulation, controlling behaviour, egoism, false-interests and duplicity.

Although engrams are 'the small print' of our inner world, they often define the parameters of our world view, our general thinking and feeling processes. Just as when one takes the time to study the small print in a contract or agreement, one often finds that the content can invalidate our expectations with regard to same; when we expose the engrams carried by a friend or, indeed, ourselves, we may sometimes be surprised or even shocked to find a belief system or world view which is narrow, artificial and pernicious.

Additionally, engrams are usually *cloaked* in individuals and not always visible from the outside. Neither are people in general always conscious of these engrams; and they sometimes jealousy guard them as cherished ideals kept from others who do not understand such views.

Engrams are usually negative in character but not exclusively so; some are positive and can add a positive dimension to an individual's psychology; such as certain types of religious beliefs. Negative engrams, however, will often retard the inner growth of a person, preventing the natural growth of humility, sincerity and justice towards others. Friendships and relationships very often fail because of engrams carried by one or both parties!

Cultural Engrams

Without deep-structured inner-work, an individual in modern society will continue to carry a well-defined number of cultural engrams.

What are cultural engrams?

These engrams, or embedded stereotyped thinking / feeling patterns, may involve such things as: prejudices, racism, double standards, self-interest, narrow judgmental thinking, undermining behaviour towards specific types of people, banal competitive manifestations, false-interests, conceit, 'the end justifies the means', 'them and us', superiority or inferiority complexes and many others too numerous to mention here.

Cultural engrams are highly visible to one who has already worked to remove them from his or her own inner psychology. <u>To those individuals coming from the same culture, these engrams remain largely invisible</u>!

Many forms of group work expose cultural engrams but, it is rare that these engrams are removed from people within these groups – intense esoteric work is often required to achieve this! (or intense psycho-spiritual work such as hypnotherapy over a period of time).

N.B. People who originate from another culture, can often see the engrams carried and manifested by individuals outside of their culture!

Many engrams are *artificial* and only serve to make a person's life more difficult. The false-ego is made up of many artificial and negative engrams, all of which only serve to blind the individual or cause great suffering, the majority of which is totally unnecessary. These engrams are all <u>imprinted mechanically</u> on the psychology of an individual through the medium of social and educational influences.

Engrams which are <u>imprinted consciously</u> using real knowledge and authentic understanding as a basis for perception are of a different order; these are created by the person's own efforts and inner work to view the cosmos and life objectively. In esotericism, they are called 'egoplasticouri'. These egoplasticouri cannot be imprinted without a certain level of cognition and effort, which is distinctly above the level of mechanical learning and cognition.

EXAMPLES OF NEGATIVE PATTERNS

- The Saboteur.
- Jealousy.
- Misogyny.
- Always being late.
- Mechanical dislike of people.
- Reacting negatively.
- Sarcasm.
- Lying.

Exercise

Make a list of your personal patterns, both positive and negative. Include all patterns you can think of, leaving out nothing. This exercise will remain at all times private – unless you wish to share items of interest with friends.

Positive Patterns

Negative Patterns

Tips For Breaking Patterns

- Firstly, isolate what patterns you wish to break.
- If necessary, consult with close confidants about this subject. Choose from your list the smallest and most insignificant item.
- Work on this item – a minimum of six weeks must be allowed to change a pattern/habit!
- If you can, substitute a positive pattern or habit in place of the old.
- Make this task 'your god' for six weeks.
- Once you have succeeded, choose the next least difficult pattern, and so on.
- Mastering small items incrementally, will generate force to deal with larger ones.
- One of the things we have direct control over is that of our attitudes. If we change our attitudes towards our life patterns and our reactions to things, we can alter a whole range of crass social and psychological programming.

  <u>We have control over our attitudes – change them!!</u>

Notes

Section 11

Adaptability

From the perspective of esotericism, adaptability is one of the most pertinent qualities one can develop in life. Another term for adaptability is to be dynamic.

We need to be able to adapt to diverse outer conditions in life and, as Gurdjieff has said, 'turn a negative situation into a positive one'. This is not an easy ability to master; it requires many qualities in the person and a great degree of real understanding.

What is adaptability built upon?

Adaptability is built upon <u>keeping the final goal in sight</u>; seeing the big picture. If we can keep the ultimate goal in sight, we can much more easily negotiate 'the stepping stones' along the way. Being dynamic is the ability to find different paths to the same destination, especially if our path is not clear or if it is blocked.

What Are The Key Elements of Adaptability?

- Risk.
- Courage.
- Adaptive thinking.
- Sensitivity / awareness.
- Foresight.
- Accepting challenges.
- Ability to move with change.
- Skill.

- Motivation.
- Having Aims.

Adaptability in Life:

Adaptability in life can mean many things: running your own business, turning a negative situation into a positive one; or becoming 'equal to life' by developing a way to make one's living in adverse conditions, and therein actually thriving.

Esotericism tells us that we must be adaptive, resourceful and dynamic in whatever life-conditions we find ourselves. Of course, this is easier said than done; not everyone will be equally adaptive. However, if we can make use of certain principles in life, it is often possible to increase our dynamic strengths and abilities to a point where we can take control of our destiny; at least in the outer world to begin with!

Principle 1 Confidence

It is important in life that we develop self-confidence; that is, the conviction that we have the skill, strength and ability to carry out the aims and tasks we set ourselves. Self-confidence comes from doing and from experience.

Principle 2 Communication

We must have the ability to communicate well with others; this can include advertising or getting our message across to an audience, a group or to our employees. We can develop communication skills over time and it is well worth the effort to do so; it will pay dividends in the end.

Principle 3 Organization

Organization skills are also very important, for if we are to do anything bigger than a day job, one will most definitely require organizational skills.

If you are lacking in organizational skills, begin by doing a small project like painting your home, inside or out. Then, undertake a small group project such as landscaping your garden or starting a vegetable-growing plot, where you involve a number of people with designated tasks to perform. You must oversee the work and intervene as appropriate to ensure its smooth running.

Other Facets to Adaptability in Society

There are other sides to adaptability, of course. These include adaptive connection to our culture or society; and adaptive connection to the core problems of Life itself (Esoteric Work).

Let us first look at how a free-thinking individual with deep vision and a strong sense of individuality, will view the key structures in our society. A person of acute perceptual vision and discernment will not be fooled by the vast array of half-truths and deceptions which are omnipresent in society.

Adaptability also means navigating and, in some cases, circumventing many of the 'false gods' in our modern society. According to esotericism, the two cardinal items in society today which have the most negative impact on us are:

1. Modern Medicine
2. Modern Education.

Modern Pharmaceutical Medicine:

Esotericism warns us about the use of modern pharmaceutical drugs. There are many sides to this phenomenon. Here, I will keep it brief and outline some of those dangers which should be obvious to all:

1. Over-prescription of these drugs in modern society.
2. Side-effects occurring with almost all modern drugs.
3. 5,000 deaths in the U.K every year from prescription drugs alone. An estimated 10,000 deaths (per year) from medical mistakes and malpractice.
4. The reliance on a chemical solution to problems which could be better treated by other means, e.g. exercise, saunas, massage, healthy diet.
5. Addiction: ever-increasing numbers of ordinary people are becoming addicted to prescription drugs.

6.   The emerging mindset which holds that an 'instant fix' must be available to them, to 'fix' their problem or illness.

7.   Invasive surgical practices which are often unnecessary.

8.   We also now have a situation where the authorities themselves estimate that as many as 10,000 people die in the U.K each year from a (medical) misdiagnosis of their illness.

9.   Many doctors, although they know the side-effects of certain drugs quite well, will not tell their patients about these side-effects!

10. Further, quite a ludicrous situation arises when a patient suffers clear side-effects from a drug prescribed by their doctor, and when they outline these side-effects at their local surgery, the doctor will often dismiss them as not being connected to the drug.

11. We now have a situation where vaccines, with dangerous contents, are been given to a wider and wider segment of the population, causing human diseases which were not even heard of a hundred years ago. People, not having the scientific knowledge with regard to the actual content and make-up of these vaccines, take them and allow their children to take them *en masse.*

Much false information is spread in the media about these vaccines and their effectiveness. The truth about vaccines has been so well hidden behind a 'smoke screen' of lies and half-truths, that the public are totally confused and often frightened into taking these medicines.

Our judgment is impaired by the powerful lobby behind modern drug companies, and multi-national companies. For instance, in the U.S.A., five billion dollars are spent each year in Washington D.C lobbying the government and Congress, by the massive pharmaceutical industry.

> *'One of the most frequent methods used to control people is to deprive them of information; if you don't know what's going on, you can't do anything about it; if people are keeping secrets from us, they are exerting power over us.'*
>
> Scilla Elworthy. (43)

Modern Education:

The problem facing modern people with regard to what they call 'education' is very complex and will require a different approach to expand upon.

Although modern education purports to bring out the best in each individual according to their abilities, this is far from true and, indeed, in centuries to come, people may well laugh and raise their eyebrows in wonderment at our ineptitude and naivety.

For a human being to develop harmoniously, it is necessary that all three parts of their being are instructed in unison. The intellectual centre, the emotional centre and moving centre must all function in harmony with one another. In modern education, the intellectual centre is the main focus of instruction, without due consideration of the emotional life of the individual or indeed the physical needs of that person.

<u>Critically authentic education, without inverted commas, must involve the instruction of all centres *together* and not in isolation</u>. That simply means that, where a person is instructed in a holistic way, all centres begin to work together *as a single mechanism!* This creates *a new dynamic* in the person, whereby, the sum of the centres becomes greater than the individual ones.

In modern life, education is seen as a means of obtaining a better position in life or acquiring wealth; not as a tool for enlarging the person themselves on an <u>internal</u> level. There is also a very real and covert sub-text to conform to the prevailing paradigm of the day, in all modern education. Tuition is fully loaded with engrams which prevail in the modus operandi of that particular culture.

And so, a type of subtle programming occurs in the individual from a very young age! Engrams are implanted in young people; and this programming will determine the individual's vision and world view thereafter; arresting the development of real intelligence, insight and *objective essence questions* in later life.

Essence development in life is thus retarded. Personality or 'the mask' carried by a man is strengthened, and the emergence of what one might call the 'pseudo-man', is perpetuated.

The masses are not aware of this hidden facet of modern education and do not study or suspect the structure of the system they are anchored in. It is rather like a fish in a fish-bowl not being aware that it is in a specific medium called water; it does not know that there is a wider world outside of its immediate watery environment and that water is helpful to its immediate life and survival but it is also a limitation.

The Missing Elements in Modern Education

We must also understand what is actually missing in our modern system of education. Below are a number of items which are pivotal to our *authentic education* for life.

- Objective principles.
- Moral Force & Psychic Force.
- Practical skills & abilities.
- Spiritual Knowledge of man's inner-potential.
- A holistic model for education.
- 'Cramming' and stress eliminated from education.
- Competition eliminated from education.
- Alternative structures and modalities of education explored.
- Students dealt with as individuals.
- An end to the 'top-down' hierarchy of instruction.
- Students should be involved in the content and design of curriculums.

In point of fact, so much is actually missing from our education system at present and so much unnecessary suffering and stress caused to students, that it is *unfit for purpose*. We are now in a situation where large numbers of students are unhappy with their education and can get no real *nourishment* for their lives through its 'barren landscape' and jaded practices.

Of course, the education system is designed to serve the State; it is not designed, in reality, to serve the individual. In many respects, there is no place in the present system for an individual. An individual who has a real knowledge of life and an insight into how education should be will find it a very limited and even alien environment. They will find themselves a participant in a fossilized and anachronistic paradigm, where the developmental needs of the individual are completely neglected!

Adaptive Connection to the Core Problems of Life

To adapt to the core problems of life, one needs to go beyond the knowledge and mind-set found in ordinary society. For extraordinary problems, supra-normal methods are required. By approaching life's problems from the esoteric perspective, we have a real opportunity to *understand* the *real meaning* of our life and the potentialities involved.

In ordinary life, meaning is subjective; for one person, it is wealth; for another, fame; for a third, status; for a fourth, hobbies; and so on. From the esoteric view of life, we place too much emphasis on externals; we become identified with the material world – with comfort, pleasure, wealth and power of various guises. We *loose ourselves* in pursuit of trivia or what can be called false-interests. What is worse, we are unaware of our trivial pursuits; we class them as important. We class ourselves as <u>very important!</u>

When we immerse ourselves in the wisdom of the ancient inhabitants of the Earth – in esoteric Knowledge – we gain a different perspective on life and on ourselves. Our perception, over time, changes. This process of changing perception, which happens slowly over time as we absorb more and more wisdom, is called *Metanoia*.

Metanoia

When this *reversal happens*, we value that which, before, was of no value; and we disregard that which we formerly valued. 'Meaning', for us, changes at a dramatic pace. We begin to view life *through the prism of our new and profound understanding!*

We begin to see into our environment on a new level and through our newly enhanced abilities, we can perceive the damage caused by the actual form and substance of how our cultures operate. The very modus operandi causes damage and suffering to vast numbers of peoples around the globe. Everything around us has an effect on us, even though in the beginning we are not aware of this because of our all pervasive conditioning.

> *'The Breeze at dawn has secrets to tell you.*
> *Don't go back to sleep.*
> *You must ask for what you really want –*
> *Don't go back to sleep.*

People are going back and forth
Across the doors where the two worlds meet;
The door is open and round,
Don't go back to sleep.'

Rumi. (44)

Notes

Section 12

Relationships

Perhaps one of the most important facets in the lives of modern peoples is that of relationships. A relationship poses a great opportunity for the inner growth of both parties; but it also creates a paradigm where almost everything is magnified to a great degree, including the small insignificant things.

In reality, a relationship should empower both parties, but this is not always what happens; we find disempowerment can often be the result! Today, more than ever before, there are problems within relationships and many relationships are breaking down. Why is this so?

When two people first meet, it is common that they meet 'on the surface' if you like, and a true meeting (essence to essence) does not take place for a number of months or even years. They are meeting 'mask to mask', and a relationship can only be successful where people meet at the core – essence to essence. Herein lays the problem. The person we meet shows us their 'better qualities'; later we begin to see their weaknesses and have doubts!

There are many potential problems facing those unwary couples who form relationships nowadays. Listed below are some of the more common issues:

- Projecting.
- Negative moods.
- The irrepressible need to change our partner.
- Loss of respect for our partner.
- Co-dependency.

- Loss of identity.
- Creating requirements.
- Control issues.
- Boundaries.
- Empowerment.
- Lack of maturity.
- Boredom.
- The False-Ego.
- Blame & Double-Standards.
- Personality disorders & 'Morphing'.

Projecting

When we enter a relationship, often we project those qualities which we might admire so much in a potential partner. These can be many and various different qualities – such as inner strength, looks, confidence, values, personality, humour, candour, courage, sincerity, prudence etc.

This projecting onto a partner or potential partner is one of those crucial elements which can later put the relationship in jeopardy, when the true qualities of the person are manifested.

Negative Moods

This is one which most people will recognize, one which is a universal problem and one which poses perhaps the greatest threat to relationships. If one's partner shows signs of continual moodiness, negative states and tantrums, this can certainly be seen as a prelude to future problems on a large scale.

With the passing of time, negative moods can 'morph' into aggression or violence. Therapy and counselling is one possible solution.

The Irrepressible Need to Change our Partner

It is very common to find that one partner will wish to change the other partner in some way, to reflect <u>how they think they should be</u>. This can sometimes be a mistake of great proportions. This new person that you may wish your partner to be or to become, over time, may well be just as subjective, and have just as many faults and failings as the former.

It is a question of acceptance. Acceptance is often key to our life and to harmonious living. There are in fact three levels of acceptance: that of ourselves; that of others; and that of our environment. This acceptance is a large part of the Byron Katie Work and is quite valuable for many people with acceptance issues.

When we are in non-acceptance mode, when we do not accept our partner as they are, we will constantly be angry, upset, frustrated and dejected. It need not be like this.

What then manifests in a relationship is stinging criticism, judgmental views and opposition on a large scale; all of which are negative and only serve to erode the fabric of any relationship.

> *When we bring in acceptance, we are coming from a much more realistic perspective.'*

> *Liz Adamson. (45)*

Loss of Respect for Our Partner

Another possibility in a relationship is the possibility of loosing respect for our partner. This loss of respect can be of many different 'colours'; but a common scenario is where one partner looses their income and the other partner then looses respect for them. This also has very interesting implications and perhaps, on occasions, throws some light on the fabric and meaning of such a relationship.

This is also part of the psychology of where one partner fundamentally sees the other *as a provider;* and this may be the *hidden core* of such a relationship. One must bear in mind that, very often, the other partner may not wish to be treated *as a provider but as a human being!*

Co-Dependency

This facet of relationships is sometimes difficult to define, but below are some of the 'tell tale' signs of co-dependency:

- No interests or hobbies, most of your time spent with your partner.
- Only feel good about yourself when you get approval.
- Constant fear of rejection.

- Your quality of life depends on the other person.
- Your entire focus in life is on the other person.
- The thought that you must be there to protect the other person always.
- Your opinions are secondary to your partner.
- All your dreams are tied up in the other person in the relationship.
- Low self-esteem.
- Self-abnegation through the denial of true feelings.
- Always compromising to suit the other person.
- Social life based entirely on the other person.
- Always deferring to the other person for answers to life problems.
- Constant controlling behaviour towards your partner.
- Self-worth only comes from problem solving, helping or soothing the other's pain.

Loss of Identity

From the perspective of self-empowerment, it is important that we maintain our sense of identity, this means also in relationships; that is, relationships of every kind.

However, it requires little research to discover that <u>many people</u> loose their sense of personal identity, very soon after entering a relationship, be it short-term or long-term. This means, in effect, that such a person becomes deeply engrossed in the other; so deeply identified, that they actually temporarily drop their own identity to a large degree.

This is not a healthy state of affairs; one should never lose one's own state of identity; this is definitive disempowerment.

Creating Requirements

Creating requirements means that, a short or medium time into a relationship, one or both parties begin to make requirements. This habit in human beings of creating requirements is a symptom of the level of their being; they wish to control, to dominate, to subjugate the other – it is a low level of behaviour and symptomatic of modern day living. We are in this behaviour, in the realm of *spoiled children* … anchored in the false-ego.

'If you are willing to look at another person's behaviour towards you as a reflection of the state of their relationship with themselves, rather than a statement about your value as a person, then you will, over a period of time cease to react at all.'

Yogi Bhajan. *[Internet quote](46)*

Control Issues

We probably all know or have known a very controlling person. They want to decide all criteria for you; where you should go and where you should not go; how you should dress and even what you might say. Sometimes parents can be in this mould.

We can also end up having a partner who fits this mould perfectly; they start to manifest controlling behaviour patterns. The underlying agenda being that of complete *compliance* with their needs, ideas, plans or schemes. Often if you do not comply, there will be tantrums, aggression, threats and possibly physical violence.

Controlling behaviour, of course, can be on various different levels; it may not be obvious at first and only later do you realize that the person is actually behaving in this fashion.

Boundaries

A cause of many problems in relationships is ill-defined boundaries and boundaries which are mutable. In other words, if we allow others to enter our private space without challenge; and by this, I mean our psychological and emotional space.

Boundaries Exercise:

You know your boundaries are weak when:

- You are always giving in to a partner.
- You blame yourself for your partner's deficiencies.
- You continually ignore your own feelings in deference to another's.

- You constantly go out of your way for your partner with no reciprocity.
- You rely financially on another.
- You feel you have to comply with another telling you what to do.
- Your friend or partner always sets the agenda.
- Your partner or friend always decides on holiday destinations.
- Your partner decides where you both live.
- Your parent's criticism deflates you completely.
- You 'dance to your parent's tune'.
- You allow your boss to touch you suggestively.
- You give in to others' demands quickly without a debate.

Your boundaries are beginning to become stronger when you notice:

- You 'keep your own counsel'.
- You no longer feel responsible for 'keeping your partner happy'.
- You don't feel guilty about your partner's problems.
- You don't take things personally.
- You do what you want to do regularly without consultation.
- Giving and receiving is easy.
- It is possible to disagree with a friend without a 'bust-up'.
- "No" is not a difficult word.
- You are comfortable 'in your own skin'.
- You can defend yourself well in any conversation.
- You don't feel obliged or threatened.
- You make decisions easily.
- You feel genuinely confident.
- You have your own agenda for life and living.

Boundary tapping to strengthen your boundaries:
    This technique serves to strengthen healthy boundaries with others in our lives and also serves to create a renewed harmony in our social life:

- Isolate a healthy boundary which you wish to create with another; i.e. 'I must not give in to my parent's unreasonable demands!'

- This is followed by tapping the boundary point, about 4 centimetres above the point of the breastbone.
- This is sometimes followed by a sensation of energy moving upwards into the throat area. If this happens, use a 'brushing movement', moving upwards from the sternum to the throat, to cleanse the negative energy and make a coughing or retching sound to aid this process. Use your fingers for this 'brushing movement' upwards and out of the body!

Empowerment

One perspective on a relationship is: whether a relationship empowers us or disempowers us. Are you empowered by your relationship with your partner or friend; or is it in fact a situation where, once it was so; but now, you may feel that it has actually reversed.

It is worthwhile to consider whether your current relationship empowers you or not. Have you lost freedoms, have you lost independence, have you lost choice and freedom of movement? Have you lost individuality; is there less joy and humour in your life? If the answer is yes, are you sacrificing some facets of life for others? For example, are you currently sacrificing certain freedoms and life qualities for security?

Many relationships are in existence through momentum only. This means that the partners concerned are *comfortable* and *secure* with their current arrangement. Many of the initial elements which initiated the relationship may have vanished but there may be many links and mutual benefits of a practical nature, which ensures the continued commitment of both parties.

Lack of Maturity

A person may be mature in years chronologically but may be immature emotionally and psychologically. This is a distinct feature of modern life.

A partner may be of the required age externally to act as a suitable partner but, internally they may be fourteen years old. This means that, in personality, they are chronologically the age they are but, in essence, they may be very much younger. This can cause great problems, consternation and anguish in many relationships.

Boredom

Another very real 'bugbear' in our modern relationships is that of old-fashioned boredom. It is something which is rarely mentioned today in relation to our marriages and partnerships. One can actually become bored with a partner.

One reason for this is where one partner continues to grow, internally, in the relationship and the other does not. It will often happen that the one who has continued to grow will become bored of the relationship.

The False-Ego

Where one or both partners have a well defined false-ego, the chances of the union surviving for a protracted period are extremely limited. Since the false-ego is essentially interested in itself and its own interests, which <u>may</u> on occasion include one's partner and extended family circle, it does not preclude egocentric behaviour patterns which serve to divide the partners.

> *'The false-ego has no desire really for truth – it desires only to support its own opinions, which to it <u>are</u> the truth, and for this purpose it will content itself with lies, distortions and half-truths …as long as they serve to keep its own view securely established.'*
>
> Jonathan Franklin. (47)

> *'One of the most common aspects of the false-ego is guilt projection. The false-ego will project its own guilt onto another and often do this very effectively. This technique of projection is very well known even to ordinary psychology.*
>
> *'This technique on the part of the false-ego has two major aspects. Firstly it casts doubt completely, on the other individual, undermining the person and secondly, it takes the attention off the false-ego and the real deception.'*
>
> Jonathan Franklin. (48)

Blame & Double Standards

As we have covered both of these before in Section 4 of our current module, I will only comment briefly on these items.

Blame and double standards are elements which today have become so engrained in our modern culture and society that they are now commonly accepted without much consternation on our part. For the most part, they have become invisible. In relationships, these elements of our psychology become more transparent and visible.

Blame:

Blame or mutual blaming in relationships is quite common. We become angry, dejected or frustrated with our partner because they have made a mistake or 'done something stupid' and we instantly BLAME!

We do not stop to think how damaging blame can be in a marriage or family unit. We even do this in front of children, which is very destructive and corrosive. It is better not to be so quick to blame, but to speak in a private area away from children and without poison in one's energy. This is not easy to do and of course requires much practice and self-restraint. It is better to do so while *being present to oneself;* or centred.

Double Standards:

This is one which is very difficult to see at first, but slowly emerges, as if from a fog to the 'clear light of day'.

For instance, we may see our partner behaving in an exemplary fashion with her own family members but she may act very differently towards ours. It may be that our partner will decry alcohol and the like in front of the children but will later drop by the pub and contradict everything thus stated.

Our partner may be 'very holistic' in nature; but later (and against mutual agreement), you may find out that they have brought the children to the clinic secretly for vaccinations.

You may have given your partner a large sum of money from your recent inheritance but, they, after having won the lottery, offer you a paltry sum.

Personality Disorders & 'Morphing'

Last but not least in this Section is perhaps of vital importance to mention in respect of its direct impact on modern relationships.

It seems that personality disorders are on the increase and they come in many 'shapes and sizes'. It is often the case that a person will find that they are in a relationship with a partner who has such a disorder.

How does this happen?

It will often happen that a person will 'mask' their illness to initiate a new relationship. It can also happen that a person will develop the disorder while <u>in</u> a relationship. Then, there is the issue of recognition; some people will not spot or recognize a personality disorder in another until it is too late.

What are the symptoms and 'tell tale' signs of a personality disorder?

The 'tell tale' signs are of the person 'morphing' or changing personality very quickly – as with Bi-Polar Disorder. There is a distinctive and real shift in the personality, where the person 'seems to be a totally different person'. In fact, for all intentional purposes, <u>they are a different person</u>. Confusion comes into the equation when they suddenly 'morph' back to their old selves and apologise for an inconvenience or just seem disorientated.

However, this is not the most difficult of scenarios. The chief difficulties arise with personality disorders that are less well defined and more difficult to spot. It may be that, for years, a partner may have 'quirks' and 'foibles' which seem to be part of the person's character but which, on further and deeper investigation, may turn out to be distinctly abnormal.

Often 'quirks' and 'foibles' are external manifestations in a person which merely hide or cloak a deeper problem. In any given country, there are perhaps many millions of people living with undetected minor personality disorders, which can and do affect the lives of those around them and, at times, profoundly affect partners and relationships.

The dynamics of a relationship depend on certain substantive issues:

- Mutual respect.
- Love & understanding.
- Intimacy.
- Trust.

- Mutual interests & aims.
- Co-operation.
- Non interference from relatives.
- A similar vision of Life –
- Acceptance –
- Compatibility

DISCUSS

Physical love depends on type & polarity, emotional love evokes the opposite and, conscious love evokes the same in response!

Gurdjieff.

The path to a successful relationship has been debated for millennia, and will probably be debated for millennia to come. However, we can see that there are definitive elements present in all good relationships. I have listed just some of them above. However, it is wise to become aware of obstacles and patterns which already exist in modern day relationships.

Things One Should Look Out For -

Double Karma Phenomena:

When we come together with a partner to form a relationship, to some degree we take on the other person's karma. This means, that to a greater or lesser degree, we take on the other persons problems, burdens etc, etc,.

Violence in Relationships:

If your partner is violent, the minimum requirement will be that you both attend co-counselling. A maximum consequence, within the relationship dynamics, will be that the oppressed partner will actively seek to leave the relationship. The most common mistake which is made by those on the receiving end of violence, is to stay in such a relationship for too long.

The Three Year Phenomenon:

This is where, after three years of being together, the initial magic which fuelled the relationship is now spent and the couple have got to work at their relationship in order to keep it alive.

Blockage & Sabotage Patterns:

Many people, after a certain time in a relationship, may begin to run blockage & sabotage patterns. That is, they begin to block their partner in certain ways or sabotage their partner's efforts in certain directions. This can often be covert or without obvious an rationale behind it, and can be bewildering to the other partner in the equation. It often remains undetected for many years into a relationship and can ultimately be the cause of a relationship ending.

Needs Not Being Met in a Relationship:

Many people engage in relationships, seeking to fulfil certain needs. It often happens that, after a period of time these needs are not fulfilled and they in turn, will withdraw from providing certain needs for their partner; feeling the need to cancel reciprocity.

An example of this is where a woman, may feel that her husband is not providing sufficient security for her, perhaps in the form of earnings or affection; she may withdraw from having sex with him as a punishment or to register her unhappiness!

Hidden Agendas:

Many hidden agendas may lie hidden behind the outward appearances of a given relationship. These can be many and varied. One such example is where a wealthy male requires a son and heir in the family but has no real interest in marriage. Marriage for him becomes a means to an end!

Lying:

You may find, after a time, to your dismay, that your partner lies a lot! This is often *bending the truth, lying by default* (not telling the whole story) and repeated small lies over a long period of time; these very small lies often serve to cloak issues just under the surface of the relationship!

Wrong Attitudes:

If your partner has a definitive problem or set of problems, and you seek to help them to change or solve their problems, you will not achieve this by being negative and abusive – this will only bring negative results and, if you persist, your partner may well leave the relationship!

Where your partner is struggling financially, negative criticism and repeated pressure will only increase their burden and difficulties – it will not help to improve the situation.

Seeking to always get your own way in a relationship is disastrous, this will cause resentment, anger and ultimately damege your relationship -

Tips for a Good Relationship

- Give your partner lots of space to grow internally & externally.
- Don't try to change your partner … advice is a different matter.
- Try not to be judgmental.
- Do not set conditions on your love or relationship!
- Do not involve friends & relatives secretly in your big decisions; this will often serve to alienate your partner.
- Let them go if your relationship sours deeply … don't cling.
- Create quality time for both you and your lover every week!
- Never criticize your partner in front of others or reveal personal matters.
- Examine your own actions and check for Double Standards – ruthless sincerity is required with this.
- Blame cautiously and never use as a weapon!
- Check for Co-Dependency issue in your relationship and start to work on these.
- Ask yourself the question: Does your relationship empower you or disempower you?
- Do you have well-defined boundaries or does your partner push you around / manipulate you? Do you push your partner around?
- Ask yourself what the relationship really means to you (meaning).

Notes

Section 13

Finding One's Gift

A problem facing most people today is the thorny issue of finding one's gift. What is 'one's gift' and how do we find it?

There are indeed many issues surrounding this subject and, in this Section, we will endeavour to look at some of the more important ones.

Finding one's gift or one's talent in life (sometimes referred to as 'one's niche') remains elusive for many people. However, it can be said that the more we are in touch with our inner-self, the more we are empowered; and the more we are empowered, the better chance we have to be connected to our real innate abilities or gifts in life.

It is often the case that an individual will have an intuitive idea of what their gifts are but, because of upbringing, custom or social pressures, will fail to follow through on their vision.

When we are free, when we are most creative, when we are tapping into new ideas in our life; this is when we are closest to discovering what our innate gift actually is! Usually, we do not have to manufacture it; we only have to somehow uncover it. Some people say that they *have no particular gift or talent;* personally, I have not found this to be true. I have never met a person yet, who has not got hidden creative talents, some of which are surprising or cloaked in some way.

The best way to discover what your hidden talent is:

The best method of discovering what your gift is: do what you are best at or what you love doing most. This may not be what you are doing for a living at present; it may be something completely different. It may be a hobby, a pastime or a special interest which you have not considered as an asset; but it often happens that what we love doing most eventually becomes our livelihood or career. The caveat being, that we may not be able to 'alter lanes' immediately; it may take some time to shift to what we actually love doing.

> *'Let yourself be silently drawn by the strange pull of what you really love. It will not lead you astray.'*
>
> *Rumi. (49)*

When we are in touch with our inner-power, our essence, we come to know very quickly, just what our talents are. So, we can see that all esoteric work actually helps us on many different levels. Getting in touch with this inner-self may sometimes take a little time and patience.

Exercise

A good exercise is to <u>visualize</u> ourselves doing the job or practice we are in tune with, and do it regularly. This creates a conduit of communication for mind and emotions. We should visualize this happening as clearly as it is possible: seeing ourselves in place, doing what we love doing best and with help from others in doing so.

One of the keys to 'growing our innate abilities' is to put more and more of our time and research into what we love doing best. By doing this, we will increase our skills, knowledge of the subject and abilities in our particular field.

Confidence

We can only gain confidence in our chosen field <u>by doing</u>; we must learn to do, and not just have a theoretical basis in what we hope to do. A 'hands-on' approach is vital to success. So, the more we get involved directly with our personal aims and goals, the more we will develop skills and abilities which will aid us to manifest our gift.

Belief in Oneself

It is also vital to have belief in oneself and, in some ways, this may come before the development of confidence. A belief in oneself will lead one to the point where we become <u>engaged</u> in our interest; and gives us the impetus and motivation to move forward and develop new confidence in various fields in life.

<u>'Swimming against the Current'</u>

Sometimes it is necessary to 'swim against the current' in life in order to follow one's dream. This is not equally easy for everyone. It can sometimes happen that a flow of circumstances happen which aid in the pursuit of one's goals. This is sometimes referred to as 'fate'. Fate basically means that you are in tune with your inner-self and thus you attract to yourself the very conditions necessary for success or for further engagement in your chosen field.

However, finding one's gift is usually a life-long endeavour; for if you were to check the private history of individuals who have succeeded in their talent or particular gift, you will probably ascertain that they have had an interest or a 'thread of activity' in their field, going back many years.

From another perspective, society is not at all interested in you finding your gift. Society is not particularly interested in empowering the individual; you must go it alone. Society creates mechanization, great pools of controlled people; society is not interested in *creating individuals*, that is, people who can *think and act for themselves*.

Self-empowerment and finding your gift are intimately linked; but you must make your own personal efforts to achieve both. When we understand more about life, more about ancient wisdom, we can then extrapolate insights into our situation which formerly were inaccessible to us. In the beginning, it is very difficult to shift from our benign and 'candy-coated' view of life – and it takes some time before we break through the veneer which separates us from *real life*.

> *'Most people today live by proxy … we do not have the courage to live for real; in today's crazy and incoherent societies, making a mistake often means a fine or jail.*
>
> *We also have a great propensity to condem, criticize, and 'pull the carpet from under others' …*

In order to live fully we have to risk: no risk – no life!

Risking makes us sharp, intelligent, aware, sensitive, to the 'micro-Vibrations' of life itself. A life without risks leaves us flat, jaded and dull. We have never lived! [The Writer – F.B. Post] [50]

Tips For Finding Your Gift

- Use this manual and course as a template for looking at personal abilities and qualities.
- Never 'put yourself down'.
- Only associate with positive people.
- Only engage with positive ideas.
- Develop a daily meditation practice.
- If you have a mentor or special teacher, listen to their advice.
- Use as many methods as you can find to develop courage.
- Try out different experiences, crafts, trades, special skills etc.
- Never give up.
- Get to know yourself well!
- Evaluate guides or teachers prudently.
- Never presume that imaginary abilities, qualities or skills are yours.
- Be prepared to learn from those *who know.*
- Develop as many useful and practical life-skills as you can.

Notes

Section 14

Integrating Male & Female Principles

The subject of integrating male and female principles internally is very old and in fact comes to us from both ancient Egypt and from Alchemy. It proposes that we join together in ourselves, the twin poles in ourselves of Yin and Yang. <u>This being one of the first steps to inner esoteric work</u>!

In the Egyptian model of inner-work, this is represented by Horus and Set. There are, of course, various layers or levels of this inner work, many of which cannot as yet be seen from our present level of development. We will however, speak of this principle in terms of its first level in us; integration, balance and inner harmony.

Before one can develop to a high spiritual level, one must first lay the basic groundwork or foundations. This means integrating the opposite principle in our psychology and our emotional cognition. That is, if we are a woman, we must develop in ourselves the masculine side of our natures and, if a man, we must develop our feminine side.

Now, this is confusing for many people because, at once, people will begin to think wrongly on this subject. A man will think that he will acquire lots of feminine traits and a woman will think that she will become very masculine – rough, aggressive, bullish, dominant etc. In fact, this is not how it works at all and nothing could be further from the truth.

<u>When we acquire the opposite pole in our inner-psycho-spiritual make-up, we are neither masculine or feminine, but transcend both</u>! Externally we retain our own gender and we can manifest our masculinity or femininity as before; but internally something has changed. <u>Our inner make-up has now become integrated</u> and we are no longer one-sided; we

are no longer viewing life from a 'one-dimensional viewpoint' but from a 'three-dimensional view'.

This is the groundwork necessary for real spiritual development and gives the individual access to latent abilities formerly out of his or her reach. From the esoteric point of view, it is incumbent on us to do this very important work on ourselves – much depends on its successful moulding into the fabric of our being. <u>Further profound work can then follow</u>!!

<u>The First Real Awareness to Manifest in Man</u>

'As a collective we are not aware that there is something very significant missing in us; in our psyche. We are so focused on money, jobs, possessions, careers, prestige, etc. that we are completely unaware of the state of our being.

We are like little children, with our entire focus on the 'candy-store', or on our 'next trip to the Zoo'. We have lost sight of what life is really all about.

Until we truly realize in our being, that there is a very significant element missing in us, material success will never plug the gap.

The status quo will remain.'

Gurdjieff Speaks to Prince Yuri Lubovedsky as a Young Man:

"Ever since I was a child, I have had the feeling that something Is missing in me, I felt that apart from my ordinary life, there Is another life, a life which is calling me – but how to be open To it?

This question never gives me any peace, and I have become like A hungry dog, chasing everywhere for an answer."

From Meetings With Remarkable Men – The Movie.

The Writer. [F.B. Post] *(51)*

The Key to Integration

The key to all of this, is that what we transcend is a limited, one-sided inner psychology; and what results, through sustained inner-work – and what is thus achieved – is a new, balanced and rounded 'emotional field'.

The advantages to this transformation in the individual are not always readily understood by people in general. It is a subtle but very tangible change in the inner-psychology of the person; a transformation which is within the reach of many people in society today.

Advantages of Change

The advantages of this process are many and varied, but I will mention some of them here for a quick reference guide:

- The ability to view the opposite sex as a human being with problems just like you! 'Them and us' disappear!
- The ability to become empathic with all genders.
- Increased awareness of one's own former position psychologically.
- Expanded communication skills.
- New awareness of problems facing both sexes, without taking sides.
- The ability to be friends with a woman, without a sexual connection, if you are a man.
- The ability to understand a man's sexuality, if you are a woman.
- For men, many new holistic and healthy friendships with women.
- A new inner-harmony for both sexes.
- A new maturity dawns with tangible benefits for the person, both inwardly and outwardly.
- Increased powers of perception.

Transcending the Duality of Sex

This maturity and inner-growth of transcending the duality of sex, as we can see from the above, enhances our abilities and inner-development. It does not mean, however, that we stop functioning as a normal man or woman. It simply means that we have developed our emotional cognition to a new high and that our Essence has begun to grow!

'You also have two polarities within you, the feminine and the masculine. Let me explain it a little in detail. Because your body is born out of two polarities – cells from your mother and cells from your father, they create your body – you have both types of cells, those which come from your mother and those which came from your father. Your body consists of two polarities, feminine and masculine. You are both, everyone is both. Whether you are a man or a woman, it makes no difference. If you are a man, you have a woman within you: your mother is there. If you are a woman, you have a man within you: your father is there. They can again meet within you. And the whole Yoga, Tantra, the alchemy, the whole process of religion, is how to create an organism, a deep intercourse, between the polarities within you. And when they meet within you, a new type of being is born, a new life form becomes alive.'

'When your inner man and inner woman meet, you are neither: you transcend sex.'

Bhagwan Shree Rajneesh. (52)

A further development in this process is that the individual becomes less focused on sex and all things sexual. A more balanced individual emerges from the old.

With this union of the male principle and female principle in a person, the individual becomes more whole, more integrated and less violent! Extremes of all varieties begin to disappear. The chakras come into a new balance and a new type of acceptance manifests where before it was absent. Acceptance of oneself, acceptance of others and acceptance of the hidden order within the Cosmos comes into being.

The Approach for a Woman

- Learning to lead and take control.
- Learning to be strong internally. For example, do not let others push you around!
- Demand equal rights with men!
- Help other women to become free of culture bound shackles.
- Develop personal resilience.
- Work at developing Courage & Tenacity.
- Learn to say No and mean it, when necessary and in diverse life situations.
- Do not be manipulated or intimidated by in-laws.
- Create and maintain strong boundaries.
- Do not neglect your fundamental female qualities such as love, care, compassion, sensitivity and tenderness.
  It is not necessary to neglect or abandon these qualities while in the process of developing courage, tenacity, resilience, confidence and self-esteem!

Measures a Woman can Undertake to Help Implement the Above

- Be unorthodox – do not accept social norms.
- Survival courses to develop confidence.
- Travel extensively – sometimes alone.
- Accept new challenges and even sometimes create them.
- Retain identity in relationships.
- Take up a spiritual practice i.e. meditation or Chi-Gung.
- Formulate your own decisions.
- Regularly set aside special time for yourself, if you are in a relationship or even have a family. The more busy you are, the greater the importance of this one!
  Start small, with say 30 minutes per week and gradually increase to say 2 hours per week; this can be two separate one hour periods!
- Question your role in society, how much of it is artificial and how much is equitable & fair?

- Curb negative moods and reactionary negative attitudes and do not self-justify; these things dis-empower you! Being positive re-routes vast amounts of psychic energy towards your personal power!
- Take up self-defence classes or similar to build confidence.
- Change you attitude from:
  'I am just a woman after all, what chance have I got!!' to
  'I am potentially as good as any person who walks this Earth!'
- Rearrange your self-image-
  'I will never accept being treated as a second-class citizen!'

The Approach for Men

- Learn to be flexible in life – rigidity is your enemy.
- Become aware of the yin-qualities you may lack, such as simplicity and compassion, sensitivity & care for others.
- Learn to have warm friendships with women without any sexual overtones.
- Understand that, allowing the yin or your female principle to flow in your own nature, means you stop suppressing it artificially into your subconscious.
- Be aware that to become *whole* and therefore more balanced, it is necessary to cultivate both the yin and yang aspects in your *Being*.
- Do not allow a culture-bound mind-set from those around you, to stop you or block you through fear.
- Work at limiting the arrogance and conceit of the ego.
- Work at going beyond logic.
- Learn a spiritual practice.
- Conquer violence and aggression in your own nature.
- Develop sincerity and humility.
- Do not neglect the masculine or yang-qualities, such as leadership, firmness, courage and 'standing your ground', while you work on creating the balancing yin-principles.

Measures a Man can Undertake to Help Implement the Above

- Cultivate reciprocity & generosity in daily life.
- Learn to play with children and put yourself psychologically and emotionally in their mind-set.
- Be gentle to all creatures and to yourself –
- Be creative, learn new creative skills which require sensitivity and feeling.
- Learn to work with your intuition.
- Develop emotional cognition and receptivity by increasing your appreciation of the best classical music and also sacred music.
- Enlarge your emotional field by learning to play a musical instrument or similar skill.
- Practice empathy with others and listening skills.
- Opening the heart-centre if absent, can be worked on through meditation, Karma Yoga and Chi-Gung practice.
- The acute awareness and disapproval of misogyny & chauvinism in others, can be a powerful tool for removing any residual elements of these in yourself -

Tips For Integrating Male & Female Principles

- Develop respect and deep insight into the opposite sex.
- Check your attitudes to the opposite sex.
- Men should show respect for women at every opportunity: women should not undermine men.
- Men need to develop their emotional intelligence & cognition: women, their intellect or mental abilities.
- Men should not be afraid to show emotions in public: women must learn to stand up for themselves and others!
- Men should learn to develop and trust their intuition: women, their ability to lead and direct.
- Co-operation should be the watchword between the sexes.
- Both sexes should develop inner-power.
- Both men and women should avoid power through domination.
- Men should conquer their aggressive tendencies; women, their propensity to manipulate others.

Notes

Section 15

Confidence & Self-Esteem

A critical element in everybody's life is that of confidence and self-esteem. Both of these elements which make up a person's character are not inborn. In other words, they are acquired during life as part of our learning and quality-building experiences. They form part of what we receive from our producers, our teachers and our peers; but also, these qualities are partly of our own making, through experience; the ability to do and to learn. Through our own efforts, we can develop confidence and self-esteem; although it is much easier, of course, if the foundations are laid in our youth by those who are responsible for creating 'the bedrock' for such development.

However, it should be noted that real confidence and healthy self-esteem lay not in Personality but in Essence.

If our confidence and self-esteem lie in Personality alone, then it is a veneer and it is shallow. If we have led a cosy, sheltered and academic life, then it is very possible that our confidence is only 'skin-deep'. It may in reality be mostly bravado. When we are really put to the test, if there is an emergency, we tend to 'fall apart'; we lack cohesion and stability at our core. Our core is 'a child', our exterior is an adult!

That is why it is necessary to <u>lead a life of action</u>; action and not academic learning builds confidence. It is interesting to note that all of the truly great teachers of old have stated this over and over again. Action is the missing link to developing real inner confidence! Yes, we need to learn, but not through pseudo-structures and false-models of learning. Our learning must be <u>holistic</u>; it must be a learning <u>which nourishes our</u>

Being and creates a new-found confidence and inner-strength; our learning must be authentic!

Therefore, we can see that, in our education system (which is academia-based), the structure is missing for the development of real confidence and self-esteem! It is also apparent that it lacks substance to endlessly study mental constructs and to learn vast amounts of largely vacuous intellectual material ad infinitum; this will not cause a young person to develop in the right way. It will only cause imbalances in the psychology and 'emotional field' of the person.

For modern man, confidence and self-esteem are intimately bound up with what surrounds him in his or her formative years. This includes the quality of those people surrounding the young person, and the quality of their (what is termed) 'Being manifestations'. These natural conditions are fundamental to the holistic and balanced development of a person.

Ready Made Answers

Unfortunately for us, our education is designed to provide us with ready-made questions and, of course, ready made answers. We cannot develop and mature as terrestrial beings, with such an artificial system of 'top down' and predetermined knowledge. As we have seen previously in this module, the knowledge we receive during the course of our 'education', is artificially put together, for purposes other than our real education.

Moulded Thinking

Our thinking parameters are moulded and limited to that of defective and logical thought, for the most part. Our innate capacity for wonder, awe and deep spiritual inspiration are retarded by outmoded methods which convey trite intellectual knowledge and substandard teaching models.

> *'The most beautiful and most profound experience is the sensation of the mystical. It is the sower of all true science. He to whom this emotion is a stranger, who can no longer wonder and stand rapt in awe, is as good as dead.*
>
> *'To know that what is impenetrable to us really exists, manifesting itself as the highest wisdom and the most radiant*

beauty which our dull faculties can comprehend only in their primitive forms; this knowledge, this feeling is at the centre of true religiousness.'

Albert Einstein. (53)

So, the first objective is to <u>free our thinking</u>. Confidence comes not only from being able to do things in life, but to 'stand apart' outside of 'the herd' and 'the herd mentality'. This requires that we open our 'inner-mind' and use our capacity to think psychologically! Only by seeing the 'big picture' as described by esoteric lore, can we begin to do this. Higher knowledge is the key.

The Psychology of Ancient Peoples

Gurdjieff tells us that the psychology of ancient peoples was different than that of today. They had the power to ponder, to contemplate profound ideas without cognitive dissonance.

'In ancient times people had the power of contemplation: that is, their mind-set was completely different than ours today. In modern times we do not contemplate: do not think for ourselves, our mind-set is made up of various elements from the societal consciousness and herd-mentality.

Should we examine our psychology and our beliefs objectively, we will find that they are made up of the very strata that are most mechanical and subjective. We will find, despite ourselves, fashionable ideas, current 'scientific' thinking, New Age ideologies, and various colourful views about ourselves which are far removed from reality.'

The Writer. *[F.B. Post](54)*

The rigidity of social norms and social programming retards Essence in us. We become *robots* by default; that is, by remaining passive, we remain as a seed – undeveloped. Opening 'the inner-mind' means engaging with our emotions and developing our emotional cognition – whereby our 'emotional field' <u>changes</u>.

<u>Emotional Anchors</u>

In order to gain something new, one must be able to release many of our old emotional anchors in society. In 'plain speak', that means re-assessing our relationship to certain mainsprings of society and to things in society which people take for granted but which are often illusions.

A good example of this is 'the must have' social syndrome, where it is now very common for large masses of people to 'buy into' a 'must have' culture. Everyone wants to own the latest shiny gadget, the newest contraption on the high street. 'Things' are now utilized to fill the gaps in our impoverished 'emotional field'. We now have to <u>possess things</u>, in order to feel good about ourselves.

Consumerism has been born; and serves to replace deeper values and principles in life. Religion has failed in its mission to nourish and serve our emotional needs; and so, since we cannot perceive anything else on the horizon which will take its place, we have turned to materialism. We are now consuming instead of *being!*

<u>Investment in Society</u>

Many people invest heavily in society, i.e. psychologically and emotionally: <u>they give their power away too easily</u>. There are many and varied facets to this paradigm. People are often very heavily identified with society and 'social norms' – such as wars, the standing of their country in the world, their leaders, politics, modern education, modern medicine, etc.

'The clock stops' when one puts the 'spotlight' on these facets of modern life and begin to re-examine their validity under the auspices of a brand new paradigm or model of perception.

To ridicule the structure of society is, for most people 'a bridge too far'.

Because of the huge emotional investment by modern people in the structure and modality of their society, it is very difficult to approach Truth. Truth is not to be found in ordinary society; only signs pointing in the direction of Truth.

Automatic Reason

There is a very strong illusion in life which supports the commonly held view that people think for themselves – it is false.

In reality, people only possess an 'automatic reason'. When we investigate this subject deeply, we find that people's opinions and their belief systems are not their own – they are all borrowed ready-made from society as an artificial construct!

One of the surprises that awaits in a deeper investigation is that it emerges that people are incredibly lazy and do not want to make the necessary efforts required for an individual to come to independent mentation and perception. And so, by and by, we find that the contents of the average person's mind, even the so called intellectuals, are utterly devoid of genuine *being-data!* Everything is 'second-hand' material, opinions, and attitudes which have never been questioned or put to the test!

This is the shameful state of modern man's mind; the contents are shallow and artificial: then lying begins – and, *lying kills Essence in us!*

Essence

Essence lives on Truth; Personality on information and gossip. To develop Essence, something more than 'education' and information is required; a new kind of *food* is required to nourish and develop Essence in us!

Truth with a capital 'T' now only exists in our 'spiritual landscape', in the form of ancient esoteric knowledge; of which, only fragments may be found in our society-at-large. It requires conscious effort on our part to distil or 'psychologically mine' more of this Truth from our surroundings, and then form it into a cohesive whole. Herein lies the chief difficulty or first major threshold: the individual who is too lazy will never investigate further!

Living by Proxy

In today's world, we tend to live by proxy. That is, we do not go on any adventure; we watch the adventure on the television or on a DVD. We go to the cinema; we go to the bar or the club; all artificial environments and all based on 'the Pleasure Principle'.

An individual cannot grow if they are to be immersed always in safety and in pleasure. In this there is no gestalt!

There is no risk involved

How can we develop real confidence and ability through living by proxy? It is not possible! Authentic living will always involve incremental risk taking!

It is only by facing the problems of life 'full on' that we can begin to grow internally; *hiding from life* cannot help us do this and remaining passive will only serve to keep us in ignorance and suffering.

We can live our lives from birth 'till death in a totally passive state, without recourse to serious thought or questioning; but this is all going to be a sheer waste. We come into the world as beggars and leave as beggars. It does not matter how much wealth we have; an individual may amass a vast fortune in a lifetime, yet still remain a beggar inside. This is because being a beggar is really an <u>internal phenomenon</u>; a psychological state.

The Challenge:

We are surrounded on every side, by crass consumerism, corruption, false-values, pseudo-religion, social real-politik, eco-destruction, government lies and secrecy; the erosion of civil liberties and a spiritual wasteland we call society! Many things we touch in life, with hope in our hearts, turn out to be fake or, in the case of people, phony individuals who let us down. After a time, a sense of helplessness sets in for many people; we grow tired in the face of this 'dense jungle'. One cannot battle forever; for we do not possess infinite energy and resources.

This is the challenge! How do we distil from life that which is valuable and leave what is mere chaff? How do we survive in a world full of illusions and deceptions?

The answer lies in our past; in the ancient teachings of our planet Earth!

Just under the surface of our 'flat society' lies a treasure trove of truly unimagined value; Knowledge & Wisdom beyond terrestrial knowledge & philosophy. It is from this 'invisible Path' that we must turn for genuine sustenance, and a sanctuary from the spiritual desert we call society.

We can gain real inspiration from this hidden wellspring of Wisdom, a reservoir to draw from in good times and times of need.

185

From the esoteric point of view, it is only from this scared Knowledge of the ancients, that we can truly learn to be whole, conquer violence in ourselves and find our true place in life. By no other means is this possible. For the third force or neutralizing force of ordinary life divides people, creates only more and more divisions, where as the neutralizing force of sacred Wisdom unites people internally and externally.

This does not mean that we should shun or fear society, for it is internally we must conduct this work but, conduct it in life and in ordinary society, without fear or hesitation; it is our birthright.

We must learn to be 'hands-on' in our life, not living from the background; not being an 'armchair-philosopher', we must learn to risk. We can only develop resilience, tenacity, courage and true confidence by being 'hands-on', by taking up the challenge of life and accepting failure along with joyous success!

Tips For Developing Confidence and Healthy Self-Esteem

- Question the status quo!
- Don't travel the path of least resistance.
- Research your life and make aims.
- Do not let others determine your actions.
- Develop objective principles for living.
- Follow your dream wherever possible.
- Accept failures but carry on regardless.
- Acting wisely in the moment is worth a thousand regrets later!
- Ask for help when you need it.
- Become independent of others as soon as possible.
- Do not dominate and do not allow others to dominate you!
- Do not accept ready-made answers to the problems of life.
- Never benefit or profit through the abject loss of others.
- Treat others as you would have others treat you.
- Set your standards high.
- Remember: you must 'walk the walk' not just 'talk the talk'!
- Develop sincerity, humility, courage and tenacity in your Being.
- Become 'heart-centred' in your thoughts and deeds!

Notes

Section 16

Conclusion

'If I were embarking upon the Way anew, my plea would be; show me how to learn and what to study. And, even before that; let me really wish to learn how to learn, as a true aspiration, not merely in self-pretence.'

Khwaja Ali Ramitani. (55)

Knowledge & Being

Man can only develop in an accelerated fashion by enlarging both his Being and his Knowledge.

One of the key elements of esoteric work is to bring our level of Being, our inner qualities and ability to do, up to the level of our Knowledge. For, in general, we know more than we can do. <u>In other words, we do not do what we know to be the right thing to do!</u>

Illusions & Unlearning

In the beginning, it is necessary to *unlearn* many things. We have numerous illusions surrounding us in our everyday lives. There are many artificial and vacuous presumptions in the lives of people; abilities and qualities which we do not possess. For instance, generally it is taken for granted that we know what knowledge is; what it actually means. This is far from the Truth!

Although we generally think that we understand what knowledge is today, we do not understand that there are different levels of knowledge. We, for instance, in general, are only familiar with terrestrial knowledge;

we are not *au fait* with esoteric knowledge or higher knowledge. We do not even understand what 'higher Knowledge' means! Because of a combination of elements in our artificial society, such as our 'education' system, man's hubris, conceit, egoism etc, high level Knowledge remains invisible to us! Man, who lives almost entirely in Personality (the mask or veneer), cannot use this instrument to perceive a Knowledge and wisdom which stands on a higher level than orthodox terrestrial knowledge.

Rationality Without Understanding

So, we can see that cold rationality without intuition and sensitivity brings only misunderstanding, conflict and stress. The critical ingredients are those of *the feminine principle;* when these are missing, we pay a very great price in society and in our personal relationships.

Much Learning Does Not Teach Understanding!

The feminine principle is often missing from our 'education' system, where there is a lack of respect for girls and for female teachers. The mind-set, of course, comes from outdated social attitudes and a world-view dominated by men (Chauvinism). With the inclusion of these qualities, a new type of awareness arises. It is not a cold and calculating reasoning; it is an awareness spliced with vision, humour, understanding, compassion and the ability to 'see the big picture'!

When we 'switch' from cold logic and rationalization, to this more holistic approach, we develop a new vision of life and a very different perspective.

The Fragmented Psyche of Modern Man

Unfortunately, modern man's psyche is, at the best of times, fragmented, untrained and entirely focused on material things. Lacking integration and cohesion, the mind of the modern man is very limited, moving between boredom and stress and then, eventually, seeking out pleasure to obliterate both.

The first sign of a good quality Being in a man or a woman is that of a responsible and decent person. The second sign of Being development in a person is that they possess a healthy dislike of the limitations presented by ordinary life. Mundane life, with all of its 'dead ends', does not satisfy this person. There is the nagging feeling of *something missing [... something more!]*:

> *'Plato himself could only give us an indirect answer: "Man is is declared to be a creature constantly in search of himself, a creature who at every moment of his existence must examine and scrutinize the conditions of his existence. He is a being in search of meaning."'*

Erich Fromm: [Beyond The Chains of Illusion]. *(56)*

The third level of Being noticeable in relation to an ordinary person, is that of an active search for 'a way out', for new knowledge.

Going Beyond Narrow Self-Interest

On the path to true self-empowerment, a question must always be asked: Are my actions from Personality or Essence?

In society, a man acts from personality; from his superficial-self. Such action is nearly always selfish in its origin and motivation.

> *'Some people will only "love you" as much as they can use you. Their loyalty ends where the benefits stop.'*

Spirit Science. *[Net Quote] (57)*

Personality and its 'poisoned-child', the false-ego, <u>are not who you are</u>. We however, take personality and the false-ego to be ourselves; a mistake on a colossal scale.

Personality is the actor on the stage of life. This personality must be made passive before any real inner-work can take place in the individual. All work which takes place while this part of our psychology is active and dominant, <u>will not be real</u>.

This work can only be done with authenticity, if we get to know ourselves – our personality. We need to begin observing ourselves.

Through careful self-observation of one's moods, attitudes, self-deception, self-justification, mechanical disliking, making silly accounts against others routinely and robotically, we can gradually develop a healthy dislike and even horror of all this negative 'inner-traffic' and begin to separate from it. This separation can only happen consciously; it cannot happen by merely wishing it!

The key to this is that we must be willing to view ourselves impartially and without a vested interest in always being right! We must view ourselves without judgment or criticism – in the beginning, <u>it is just seeing</u>!

Core Elements to Self-Empowerment

- Find your Gift.
- Develop personal Inner-Power.
- Cleanse your emotional centre.
- Develop assertiveness / speak your truth.
- Engage your ability for psychological thought.
- Always consider externally.
- Open the heart-centre.
- Work on your false-ego.
- Develop the four powers of Essence:
- Sincerity, Humility, Courage and Tenacity.
- Develop a love of Knowledge & ancient wisdom of the Earth.
- Be resourceful in life.
- Be reciprocal.
- Free yourself from the opinions of others – the first liberation.
- Identify lying and self-deception in oneself.
- Be aware of your 'comfort-zone' and how it limits you!
- Develop <u>coherent</u> aims in your life.
- Take back your power from others and from situations / society's professionals!
- Do not dominate nor allow yourself to be dominated.
- Practice Karma Yoga.
- Create authentic meaning in your life: this can be a layered phenomenon and take time (the analogy of the onion).
- Practice meditation.
- Use the 'Spiritual Autopsy'.
- Become aware of the many illusions that surround you.

- Integrate the male and female principles within oneself.
- Defeat violence in oneself.
- Learn to relax both the body and the nervous system.

'Stepping into the Fire'

The average person is made up of a vast amount of unfulfilled potential. A person carries numerous gifts and talents internally but very often, like a 'Pandora's Box' of many compartments, these hidden abilities and qualities are never accessed.

The key to life is accessing these hidden gifts and abilities! Empowerment is the ability to access these inner-powers. When a person becomes directly connected to their own inner-power, they become catalysts for others to do the same! They become like beacons on the horizon of a 'spiritual desert'.

Pitfalls on the Path to Self-Empowerment

- I already know!
- Is this a cult?
- External-empowerment without internal-empowerment.
- Internal-empowerment without external-empowerment.
- I am too attached to my 'comfort zone'.
- I don't have any hidden gifts or abilities!
- I have always lived in Essence.

I already know!

There are many reasons why one might not recognize what empowerment means; chief among these is ignorance ... I already know; I have nothing to learn.

Is this a cult?

The subject of how esotericism has become related to the subject of cults is very important.

In the 1960's through to the 1980's, many groups and weird organizations all over the world began to borrow ideas and concepts from a few authentic sources and began to mix them with ideas taken from eastern religions and cutting-edge western psychology; groups were formed where these ideas were expounded and taught in various different formats. People were attracted to these groups and organizations worldwide, thousands of people joined seeking fulfilment, enlightenment or just new ideas. The age of the cult had arrived.

Many people were duped, some believed they had received valuable instruction for life; which some probably did. However, because many esoteric ideas were borrowed from authentic sources and mixed with other dubious concepts, many authentic esoteric ideas became clouded and 'soiled' in the minds of people. This later led to a mass distrust of all such ideas, good and bad; valid and invalid.

All new ideas along these lines are now considered to come from such cults and viewed with distrust and fear!

Esoteric ideas, of course, exist outside of all such activity and have existed for millennia. All true Knowledge has three definitive aspects: a practical side, a philosophical side and a theoretical side. Esoteric wisdom cannot be used in a diluted form in this way; it can only have negative results with few exceptions.

External-empowerment without internal-empowerment

It is, of course, possible to achieve outer success in life without any inner development or inner-empowerment. In this case, we may achieve outer acclaim but ultimately still remain empty inside. (Tolstoy's story)

Inner-empowerment without external-empowerment

This one is very common. Many people who have some success at working on themselves and developing balanced personal power, fail to achieve any kind of 'traction' in their outer life.

I am too attached to my 'comfort zone'

Clinging to our 'comfort zone' will only result in failure, with regard to our real unfoldment as human beings.

I don't have any hidden gifts or abilities!

My personal opinion is, from observation and experience over the years, that each and every person <u>has</u> hidden talents. The key is in how we bring our talents 'to the surface'.

<u>I have always lived in Essence!</u>

The truth is that it is very rare to find a person in our Western world, who lives entirely in their Essence.

In the beginning, the best combination for inner-work is an equal development of Essence and Personality. It must always be remembered that it is the norm in the majority of people to find that Essence is, in reality, immature and childish; therefore it is necessary to work on Essence and bring about its maturation, awareness and strength!

Final Comment

We live in a time of change, insecurity, loss of identity, superficial values and exploitation. Mental illness and drug abuse (both legal and illegal) are now reaching epic proportions.

Our spiritual legacy has become lost to us and we have become cut-off from our true roots. People now live in the most superficial part of themselves, having lost touch with the core of their Being and the true meaning of their existence.

Even the word *spiritual* has lost all meaning for most people, since it has become used and abused so much in recent times. It is now necessary to rediscover the <u>true meaning</u> of the word *spiritual* and to fathom just how much it has departed from its true substance.

<u>Empowerment:</u>

This is a vague term in some respects; it has many variations and guises. In real terms, however, it relates to our inner-world; how we truly feel about ourselves, our confidence, well-being and sense of identity. It is very easy to mistakenly feel that we are already empowered; it is easy to mistake external material success for inner-empowerment.

Obviously, empowerment is a <u>layered phenomenon</u>, which incrementally we develop internally, and liberate ourselves both externally and from the false-ego, in stages.

This manual should be used as a source book for such work: a sort of fluid and lucid template for changing our life, from the inside-out!

In some cases, it may be that some individuals with life problems, perhaps emotional or psychological, may require healing or therapy / counselling, prior to this kind of undertaking.

It now only remains for me to wish you every success in your personal work and life path, to increased freedom and empowerment!

> *'Deep in the Sea*
> *lie treasures beyond belief;*
> *but if you seek safety*
> *you will find it on the shore!'*

> *Saadi. (58)*

Notes

Recommended Reading

- *In Search of the Miraculous*, P.D. Ouspensky.
- *Psychological Commentaries*, Maurice Nicoll.
- *Free to be Human*, David Edwards.
- *What Doctors Don't Tell You*, Lynne McTaggart
- *The Fourth Way*, P.D. Ouspensky.
- *Conscience: The Search for Truth*, P.D. Ouspensky.
- *A Woman's Herbal*, Kitty Campion.
- *Our Life With Mr.Gurdjieff*, Thomas & Olga De Hartman.
- *Meetings With Remarkable Men*, G.I. Gurdjieff.
- *Life Is Real Only Then When 'I Am'*, G.I. Gurdjieff.
- *Views From the Real World*, G.I. Gurdjieff.
- *All and Everything*, G.I. Gurdjieff.
- *Life Between Having and Being*, Eric Fromm.
- *The Art of Being*, Eric Fromm.
- *The Joy of Living Dangerously*, Bagwan Shree Rajneesh.
- *The Hidden Harmony*, Bagwan Shree Rajneesh.
- *The Supreme Doctrine*, Bagwan Shree Rajneesh.
- *The Unknowable Gurdjieff*, Margaret Anderson.
- *Transform Stress Into Vitality*, Mantak Chia.
- *Teachings of Gurdjieff*, C.S. Nott.

Glossary

1. Maurice Nicoll.   Psychological Commentaries.
2. Maurice Nicoll.   Psychological Commentaries.
3. Maurice Nicoll.   Psychological Commentaries.
4. P.D. Ouspensky.   In Search of the Miraculous.
5. Maurice Nicoll.   Psychological Commentaries.
6. Maurice Nicoll.   Psychological Commentaries.
7. Maurice Nicoll.   Psychological Commentaries.
8. Maurice Nicoll.   Psychological Commentaries.
9. Hadrat Munuidin Chisti.   The Way of the Sufi (Idres Shah).
10. Maurice Nicoll.   Psychological Commentaries.
11. Alfred Richard Orage.   Student of Gurdjieff.
12. Simon and Garfunkel.   Bridge Over Troubled Waters.
13. Maurice Nicoll.   Psychological Commentaries.
14. Maurice Nicoll.   Psychological Commentaries.
15. Saadi.   The Rose Garden.
16. Maurice Nicoll.   Psychological Commentaries.
17. Maurice Nicoll.   Psychological Commentaries.
18. Alfred Richard Orage.   Student of Gurdjieff.
19. Ching Fang Chang.   Thesis on Museum Studies.
20. Ching Fang Chang.   Thesis on Museum Studies.
21. Ching Fang Chang.   Thesis on Museum Studies.
22. David Edwards.   Free to be Human.
23. Osho.   Morning Contemplation.
24. Liz Adamson.   12 Steps to Happiness.
25. J.T.   Wishes to remain Anon.
26. P.D. Ouspensky.   In Search of the Miraculous.
27. Maurice Nicoll.   Psychological Commentaries.
28. Maurice Nicoll.   Psychological Commentaries.
29. Harry Benjamin.   On Krishnamurti & Gurdjieff.

30. Maurice Nicoll.   Psychological Commentaries.
31. Maurice Nicoll.   Psychological Commentaries.
32. Idres Shah.   The Way of the Sufi.
33. Maurice Nicoll.   Psychological Commentaries.
34. Maurice Nicoll.   Psychological Commentaries.
35. Maurice Nicoll.   Psychological Commentaries.
36. Patanjali.   Unknown Publication.
37. Idres Shah.   The Way of the Sufi.
38. David Edwards.   Free to be Human.
39. Liz Adamson.   12 Steps to Happiness.
40. Idres Shah.   The Way of the Sufi.
41. Maurice Nicoll.   Psychological Commentaries.
42. Liz Adamson.   12 Steps to Happiness.
43. Scilla Elworthy.   Power & Sex.
44. Jalaluddin Rumi.   Publication unknown to me.
45. Liz Adamson.   12 Steps to Happiness.
46. Osho.   The Joy of Living Dangerously
47. Jonathan Franklin.   Mind & Relationships
48. Jonathan Franklin.   Mind & Relationships.
49. Jalaluddin Rumi.   Publication unknown to me.
50. Maurice Nicoll.   Psychological Commentaries.
51. Maurice Nicoll.   Psychological Commentaries.
52. Bagwan Shree Rajneesh.   The Supreme Doctrine.
53. Albert Einstein.   Publication unknown to me.
54. Maurice Nicoll.   Psychological Commentaries.
55. Idres Shah.   The Way of the Sufi.
56. Maurice Nicoll.   Psychological Commentaries.
57. Maurice Nicoll.   Psychological Commentaries.
58. Saadi.   The Rose Garden.

About The Author

The author currently lives in London, U.K, but hails originally from Donegal in Ireland. A life-long student of esotericism and the arcane, Mr McKeaney is also a fully trained holistic counsellor and therapist - specializing in hypnosis.

Having given numerous lectures and workshops on the subject of esoteric wisdom and lost knowledge in London, he has decided to render into print, all of his experience, insights and understanding of G.I. Gurdjieff's materials, for the edification of contemporary readers.

This he sees as one of the focal tasks of his life, and partly the reason for the current volume on self-empowerment.

Mr McKeaney discovered he had a natural ability and gift for understanding and subsequently articulating his insights to others: both in written and lecture form.

Further esoteric materials are about to be released on this perennial and powerful subject - in due course. Future materials will put in the public domain, numerous ideas and arcanum formerly left vague and abstruse.

Printed in the United States
By Bookmasters